Prepare for Grade 5

Second Edition

Summertime Learning

Prepare Your Child for Fifth Grade

Directions in Spanish and English

I0806960

Editorial Project Manager
Eric Migliaccio

Editor in Chief
Brent L. Fox, M. Ed.

Creative Director
Sarah M. Fournier

Cover Artist
Diem Pascarella

Illustrators
Mark Mason
Renée Mc Elwee

Art Coordinator
Renée Mc Elwee

Imaging
Amanda R. Harter

Publisher
Mary D. Smith, M.S. Ed.

Teacher Created Resources
12621 Western Avenue
Garden Grove, CA 92841
www.teachercreated.com

ISBN: 978-1-4206-8098-0

Reprinted, 2022 (PO604259)

Made in U.S.A.

Teacher Created Resources

Table of Contents

Table of Contents *(cont.)*

An Important Message

El siguiente es un mensaje importante de la Asociación Nacional de Aprendizaje de Verano.

Estimados padres,

¿Sabían que todos los jóvenes experimentan una pérdida de aprendizaje cuando no participan en actividades educativas durante el verano? Esto significa que parte de lo aprendido durante el año escolar suele evaporarse durante los meses de verano. Sin embargo, la pérdida de aprendizaje se puede prevenir con la ayuda de los padres. El verano es la época ideal para participar en actividades interesantes y divertidas que ayuden a los niños a conservar y desarrollar sus habilidades académicas. Algunas ideas:

- Lean con sus hijos a diario. Visiten juntos la biblioteca local y escojan libros que aborden temas de su interés.
- Pidan a los docentes recomendaciones para la lectura de verano. The Summer Reading List (páginas 92–94 de esta guía) constituye un buen punto de partida.
- Exploren parques, reservas naturales, museos y centros culturales.
- Consideren cada día como un sinfín de posibilidades de aprendizaje. Medir las cantidades en una receta o estudiar un mapa antes de un viaje en auto constituyen algunos modos de adquirir o reforzar una habilidad. Utilicen las Learning Experiences que se encuentran al final de este libro para obtener más ideas.
- Establezcan metas a alcanzar de forma diaria. Por ejemplo, realizar cinco problemas de Matemáticas o leer un capítulo de un libro.
- Alienten a su hijo a completar las actividades de los libros tales como *Summertime Learning*, con el fin de reducir la brecha de aprendizaje que suele producirse en el verano.

Nuestra visión es que cada niño se sienta seguro, saludable y comprometido con el aprendizaje durante el verano. Para obtener más información, diríjanse a *www.summerlearning.org*.

¡Que pasen un verano *memorable*!

Matthew Boulay
NSLA Founder

Using This Book

Como padre, posiblemente sepas que el verano es una época para divertirse. Pero también puede ser un tiempo para aprender y prepararse para el próximo año escolar. Al combinar la diversión con el aprendizaje, los libros incluidos en la serie *Summertime Learning* pueden ayudar a tu hijo a mantenerse en el camino educativo y, a su vez, disfrutar del descanso físico y mental que tanto necesita. Con el fin de ayudarte a ayudarlo, hemos desarrollado un recurso organizado, flexible, práctico y gratificante.

Organizado

Summertime Learning: Prepare Your Child for FIfth Grade se encuentra organizado en torno a un período vacacional de ocho semanas. Incluye dos actividades para cada día de la semana. De lunes a jueves, dichas actividades consisten en una lección de Matemáticas y una lección de lectura o escritura. Los viernes ofrecen un divertido cambio de ritmo e incluyen actividades que se centran en habilidades tales como la creatividad, el pensamiento crítico, la capacidad de seguir instrucciones y la resolución de problemas.

Flexible

Hay muchos modos de utilizar este libro de forma efectiva:

- **Día a día**—Tu hijo puede realizar las actividades en orden, comenzando el primer lunes de las vacaciones. Para cada día de la semana, realizará las dos actividades designadas. (Consulta el calendario de la página 7).
- **A elección**—Si no quieres que tu hijo realice las actividades estrictamente en el orden en que están presentadas en el libro, puedes elegir una combinación de páginas acorde con sus necesidades e intereses.
- **De todo tipo**—Si sientes que tu hijo necesita más apoyo en un área que en otra, puedes optar por centrarte en las actividades de Matemáticas o Artes del Lenguaje.

Además, las páginas de este libro se encuentran perforadas, lo que permite arrancarlas en caso de ser necesario. Si se escoge este método, se puede decorar una carpeta y designarla especialmente para almacenar las páginas sueltas.

Extra Extra

- Para acceder a un práctico calendario que ayude a establecer expectativas y mantenerse al día, consulta la página 7 de este libro.

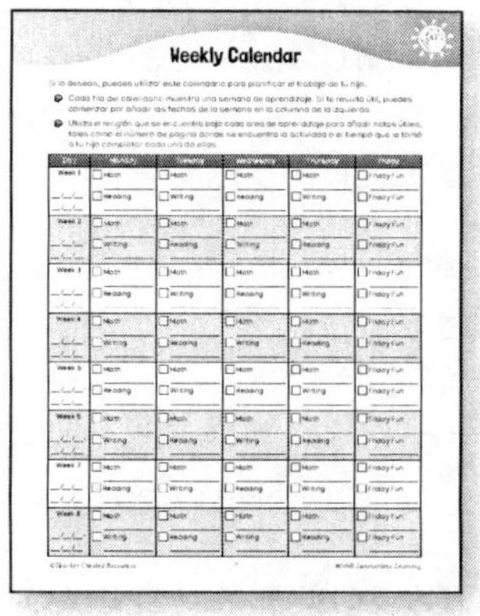

- Para incluir más escritura en el programa semanal, consulta los "Journal Topics" en la página 8.
- Para conocer distintos modos de incrementar la lectura de verano y las experiencias de aprendizaje, consulta las páginas 92–97.
- Para páginas de referencia útiles en las áreas de escritura cursiva, multiplicación, división y más, consulta las páginas 98–104.

Práctico

Los padres desean páginas de actividades que no generen dudas sobre cómo utilizarlas, qué se espera que su hijo haga, y cuáles son las respuestas correctas. Las páginas de *Summertime Learning: Prepare Your Child for Fifth Grade* tienen como objetivo responder a esta necesidad.

En la parte superior de cada página de actividades se ofrecen distintos datos de forma directa y de fácil lectura.

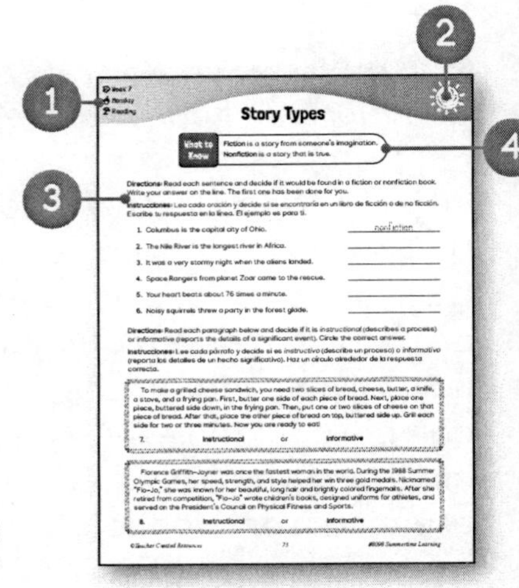

1. En un costado de la página de actividades, se encuentran el día de la semana y el área de aprendizaje. Esto permite a los padres verificar rápidamente en qué se encuentra trabajando su hijo y mantenerse organizados a lo largo del verano.

2. En el costado opuesto de la página figura un ícono de un sol. Constituye el sitio ideal para colocar una calcomanía y, de esta forma, hacer un seguimiento del progreso de tu hijo y recompensarlo cuando completa las actividades incluidas en el libro. Esta función también ayudará a orientarlo hacia las actividades del día siguiente. Al final del libro, encontrarán más de 300 calcomanías coloridas que podrán ser utilizadas para este fin.

3. Las instrucciones para cada una de las actividades se encuentran escritas de forma clara y de un modo que permita comprenderlas fácilmente. Muchas veces sucede que los niños poseen la capacidad de desempeñar una habilidad educativa, pero responden de modo incorrecto porque las instrucciones no son lo suficientemente claras o no han sido leídas en su totalidad.

4. Algunas páginas incluyen un casillero llamado "What to Know" que ofrece un recordatorio de la regla gramatical u ortográfica que tu hijo deberá saber para poder completar la página.

Además, al final del libro se incluye una guía completa de respuestas (páginas 105–111) que puede ser consultada cada vez que se tengan dudas sobre alguna respuesta.

Recompensas

Puedes utilizar el Reward Chart que se encuentra en la página 112 de este libro para realizar un seguimiento de aquellas actividades que ya han sido completadas. Esta página está diseñada para ser utilizada con las calcomanías proporcionadas al final de este libro. Cada vez que tu hijo finalice una página, puede escoger una calcomanía y utilizarla para rellenar uno de los círculos del gráfico.

Las calcomanías también pueden ser utilizadas en las páginas individuales. El sol que se encuentra en la parte superior de la página constituye el sitio ideal para colocar la calcomanía escogida. De este modo, será más fácil orientarlo hacia las actividades del día siguiente: pueden simplemente localizar la última calcomanía colocada y trabajar en las dos páginas consecutivas.

Weekly Calendar

Si lo deseas, puedes utilizar este calendario para planificar el trabajo de tu hijo.

- Cada fila del calendario muestra una semana de aprendizaje. Si te resulta útil, puedes comenzar por añadir las fechas de la semana en la columna de la izquierda.
- Utiliza el renglón que se encuentra bajo cada área de aprendizaje para añadir notas útiles, tales como el número de página donde se encuentra la actividad o el tiempo que le tomó a tu hijo completar cada una de ellas.

Day	Monday	Tuesday	Wednesday	Thursday	Friday
Week 1 __/__/__- __/__/__	☐ Math ________ ☐ Reading ________	☐ Math ________ ☐ Writing ________	☐ Math ________ ☐ Reading ________	☐ Math ________ ☐ Writing ________	☐ Friday Fun ________ ☐ Friday Fun ________
Week 2 __/__/__- __/__/__	☐ Math ________ ☐ Writing ________	☐ Math ________ ☐ Reading ________	☐ Math ________ ☐ Writing ________	☐ Math ________ ☐ Reading ________	☐ Friday Fun ________ ☐ Friday Fun ________
Week 3 __/__/__- __/__/__	☐ Math ________ ☐ Reading ________	☐ Math ________ ☐ Writing ________	☐ Math ________ ☐ Reading ________	☐ Math ________ ☐ Writing ________	☐ Friday Fun ________ ☐ Friday Fun ________
Week 4 __/__/__- __/__/__	☐ Math ________ ☐ Writing ________	☐ Math ________ ☐ Reading ________	☐ Math ________ ☐ Writing ________	☐ Math ________ ☐ Reading ________	☐ Friday Fun ________ ☐ Friday Fun ________
Week 5 __/__/__- __/__/__	☐ Math ________ ☐ Reading ________	☐ Math ________ ☐ Writing ________	☐ Math ________ ☐ Reading ________	☐ Math ________ ☐ Writing ________	☐ Friday Fun ________ ☐ Friday Fun ________
Week 6 __/__/__- __/__/__	☐ Math ________ ☐ Writing ________	☐ Math ________ ☐ Reading ________	☐ Math ________ ☐ Writing ________	☐ Math ________ ☐ Reading ________	☐ Friday Fun ________ ☐ Friday Fun ________
Week 7 __/__/__- __/__/__	☐ Math ________ ☐ Reading ________	☐ Math ________ ☐ Writing ________	☐ Math ________ ☐ Reading ________	☐ Math ________ ☐ Writing ________	☐ Friday Fun ________ ☐ Friday Fun ________
Week 8 __/__/__- __/__/__	☐ Math ________ ☐ Writing ________	☐ Math ________ ☐ Reading ________	☐ Math ________ ☐ Writing ________	☐ Math ________ ☐ Reading ________	☐ Friday Fun ________ ☐ Friday Fun ________

Journal Topics

Haga que su hijo elija uno de estos temas del diario dos veces por semana. En un diario o cuaderno, pídales que escriban algunas oraciones en respuesta al tema elegido. Recuérdeles que agreguen suficientes detalles para que otra persona que lea sus respuestas sepa lo siguiente sobre su tema:

Quién   Qué   Cuándo   Donde   Por qué   Cómo

Si lo deseas, puedes utilizar lo siguiente como herramienta de organización. Marca la fecha en que tu hijo completó cada consigna.

#1 the city or place I would most like to visit Completed: ______	#2 the perfect pizza Completed: ______	#3 my favorite singer or musical group right now Completed: ______
#4 the most interesting TV show or film I have seen lately Completed: ______	#5 how neat (or not neat) of a person I am Completed: ______	#6 the importance (or unimportance) of daily exercise Completed: ______
#7 what it takes to become a great artist or musician Completed: ______	#8 what I would tell a 3rd grader at my school about 4th grade Completed: ______	#9 the one school subject I would study all day if I could Completed: ______
#10 a funny experience I recently had Completed: ______	#11 a fight or argument I recently had Completed: ______	#12 the reasons why a 5th grader should (or should not) get an allowance Completed: ______
#13 what a perfect summer day would be Completed: ______	#14 why I would (or would not) like to be a doctor Completed: ______	#15 the one thing I would most want to save my money to buy Completed: ______
#16 my favorite type of pet Completed: ______	#17 what it takes to be a good friend Completed: ______	#18 my favorite athlete to watch compete in sports Completed: ______

Standards and Skills

Estándares Educativos

Cada una de las actividades incluidas en *Summertime Learning: Prepare Your Child for Fifth Grade* cumple con uno o más de los estándares educativos nacionales. Para conocer cómo se relacionan específicamente las actividades con los estándares básicos estatales, visita *http://www.teachercreated.com/standards.*

- Desplázate hacia abajo en la lista alfabética para encontrar la *Summertime Learning (2nd Edition)* series.
- Haz clic en **Standards** el link para acceder a TCR8845 Summertime Learning Grade 5 Standards.

Habilidades Introducidas y Reforzadas

Las actividades de *Summertime Learning: Prepare Your Child for Fifth Grade* tienen como objetivo reforzar las habilidades aprendidas el cuarto grado, así como introducir otras nuevas que luego serán desarrolladas el quinto grado. Dichas habilidades se encuentran enumeradas a continuación, y en la página 10–11.

Escritura

- Utiliza estrategias de escritura para muchos propósitos y contextos
- Utiliza estrategias para redactar, revisar y corregir trabajos escritos
- Escribe un texto explicativo
- Escribe un texto narrativo
- Escribe un texto autobiográfico
- Escribe en respuesta a textos de no ficción
- Escribe en respuesta a textos de ficción
- Utiliza lenguaje descriptivo para mejorar las ideas
- Escribe oraciones completas cuando se indica
- Utiliza la forma de párrafo por escrito cuando se indica
- Utiliza una variedad de estructuras de oraciones en el trabajo escrito
- Usa varias partes del discurso, incluidos sustantivos, pronombres, verbos, adjetivos, adverbios y conjunciones—en el trabajo escrito
- Usa correctamente la ortografía, el uso de mayúsculas y puntuación en composiciones escritas
- Evalúa la escritura propia y la de los demás

Habilidades Introducidas y Reforzadas *(cont.)*

Lectura

- Previsualiza el texto
- Establece un propósito para la lectura
- Hace predicciones simples sobre lo que se encontrarás en un texto y confírmalas/revísalas predicciones cuando sea necesario
- Utiliza claves fonéticas y estructúralas para decodificar palabras desconocidas
- Usa claves sintácticas y contextuales para decodificar palabras desconocidas
- Entiende el vocabulario de lectura apropiado para el nivel
- Comprende patrones estructurales u organización en textos informativos
- Hace modificaciones a las estrategias de lectura según sea necesario
- Ajusta la velocidad de lectura para adaptarse al propósito y al nivel de dificultad del material
- Utiliza organizadores de texto para determinar la idea principal y otros elementos textuales
- Entiende el concepto de trama
- Entiende el propósito o el punto de vista del autor
- Conoce las características definitorias de una variedad de formas y géneros literarios
- Comprende y aplica el concepto de causa y efecto
- Hace inferencias o saca conclusiones basadas en la caracterización
- Resume y parafrasea información en textos
- Hace conexiones entre los eventos de las historias y las experiencias personales

Matemática

- Utiliza muchas estrategias para comprender los problemas
- Entiende que la manera de representar un problema puede ayudar en la solución del problema
- Conoce el lenguaje de operaciones básicas
- Utiliza prueba y error para resolver problemas
- Conoce la diferencia entre información relevante e irrelevante al resolver un problema
- Comprende los conceptos básicos de la teoría de los números

Standards and Skills *(cont.)*

Habilidades Introducidas y Reforzadas *(cont.)*

Matemática (cont.)

- Entiende formas equivalentes de porcentajes, fracciones y decimales
- Entiende el lenguaje de las operaciones básicas
- Entiende el significado básico del valor posicional
- Entiende la relación básica entre números enteros, fracciones, decimales y números mezclados
- Comprende las relaciones entre la suma, la resta, la multiplicación y la división
- Usa modelos para identificar, ordenar y comparar números
- Multiplica y divide números enteros ccorrectamente
- Suma, resta, multiplica y divide decimales correctamente
- Suma y resta fracciones simples correctamente
- Usa estrategias para estimar cálculos
- Realiza cálculos mentales básicos
- Determina el efecto de la suma, resta, multiplicación y división en el tamaño y orden de los números
- Resuelve problemas del mundo real que incluyen operaciones numéricas
- Selecciona y utiliza las herramientas apropiadas para las tareas de medición
- Utiliza estrategias específicas para estimar cantidades y medidas
- Conoce el lenguaje básico para describir y nombrar formas geométricas
- Entiende las propiedades básicas de las figuras
- Entiende que las formas pueden ser congruentes o similares
- Comprende las características de las líneas y los ángulos
- Utiliza la geometría de movimiento para comprender las relaciones geométricas
- Resuelve oraciones abiertas simples que involucran operaciones con números enteros
- Entiende que las ideas y los conceptos matemáticos se pueden representar gráficamente
- Sabe que una variable es una letra o símbolo que se usa para representar uno o más números
- Utiliza gráficos de barras, gráficos circulares y gráficos de líneas simples para organizar datos y hacer comparaciones

Pay and Play

Directions: Solve each problem using multiplication or division. Show your work.

Instrucciones: Resuelve cada problema usando multiplicación o división. Muestra tu trabajo.

1. If one football costs $21.45, how much would nine footballs cost?

Nine footballs would cost ____________.

2. A group of seven parents rented a giant bouncer for $84.63. They split the cost evenly. How much did each parent pay?

Each parent paid ____________.

3. A bag of jacks cost $2.79 at the toy store. How much would it cost for 30 bags?

Thirty bags would cost ____________.

4. A basketball team bought a hoop and rim for $59.95. If the five players split the cost evenly, how much did each player pay?

Each player paid ____________.

5. A bag of marbles cost $2.79. A group of five teachers bought 20 bags of marbles and split the cost evenly. How much did each teacher pay?

Each teacher paid ____________.

6. A checkerboard game costs $12.50 at the Great Games store. How much would it cost to buy 20 checkerboard games?

Twenty checkerboard games would cost ____________.

The Blink of an Eye

Directions: Read the story and look at the chart that goes with it. Use them to answer the questions below.

Instrucciones: Lee la historia y mira el gráfico que la acompaña. Úsalos para responder a las preguntas a continuación.

Have you ever tried to stare at something without blinking? Don't try too hard! Blinking serves several important purposes.

For one, blinking provides moisture to the surface of your eyeball. Without this moisture, your eyeball will feel dried out. Your vision may suffer. Also, blinking actually cleans your eyeball. Tiny particles of dust and other foreign objects are constantly landing on the surface of your eye. As you blink, the up-and-down motion of your eyelids wipes these things away.

The following chart shows how often three different groups of people blink their eyes over certain periods of time.

Number of Minutes	1	5	10	60
Average person	15	75	150	900
Baby or infant	2	10	20	120
Person using a computer	7	35	70	420

1. Restate what you learned from reading the article. What are two ways in which blinking is helpful?

   a. ______________________________

   b. ______________________________

2. Use the chart to answer these questions. How many times would . . .

   a. the average person blink in 5 minutes? ______________

   b. a person using a computer blink in 10 minutes? ______________

   c. a baby or infant blink in 30 minutes? ______________

3. From the information given, what can you infer are the effects of computer use on a person's eyeballs? Use the story and the chart to back up your answer.

   ____

   ____

   ____

Spending Money

Directions: Ginger receives an allowance of $10 per week. The pie chart shows how Ginger spends her money.

Instrucciones: Ginger recibe una asignación de $10 por semana. El gráfico circular muestra cómo Ginger gasta su dinero.

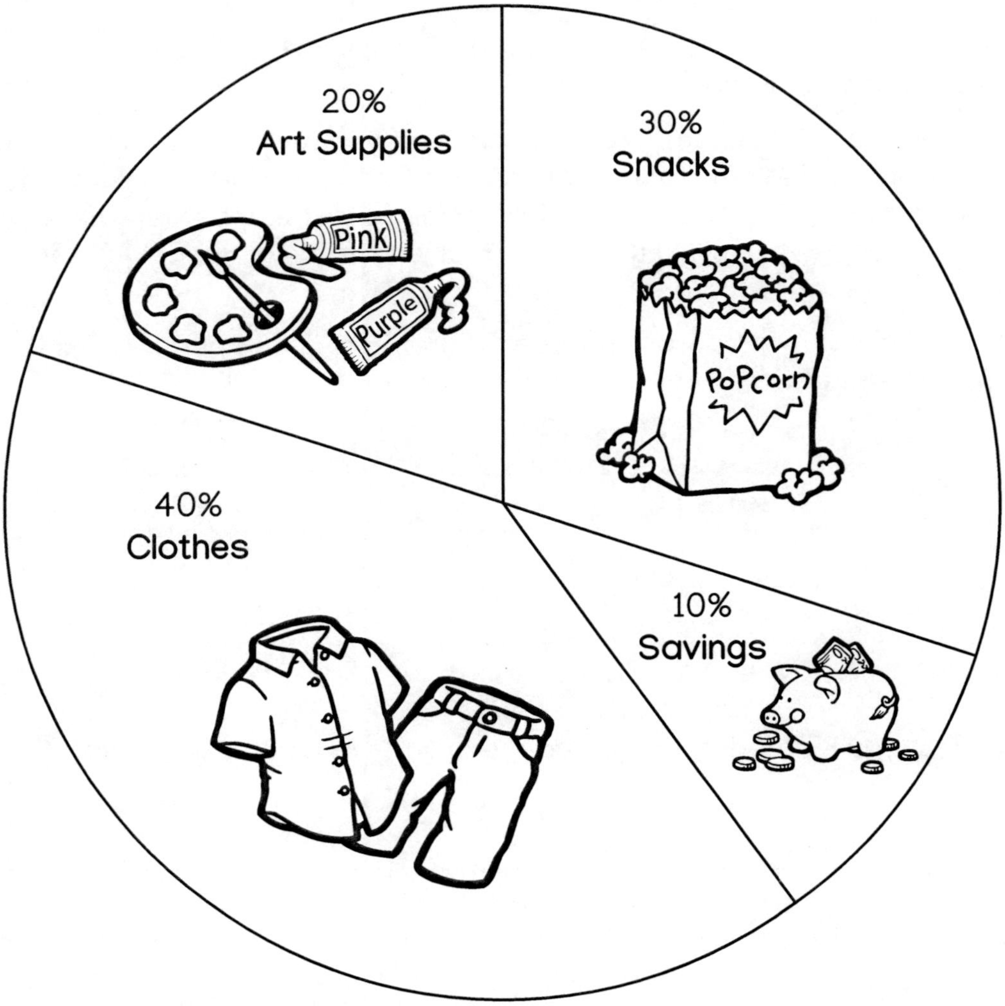

1. How much money does Ginger spend on each category of items in one week?

   Art Supplies: ____________________ Snacks: ____________________

   Clothes: ____________________ Savings: ____________________

2. If the average month has 4 weeks, how much money does Ginger save in a month? ____________________

3. A year has 52 weeks. How much money does Ginger spend on art supplies in a year? ____________________

4. If Ginger uses her clothes money to buy a $25 coat, how many weeks will it take her to fully pay for it? ____________________

The Main Idea

Directions: Read the following paragraph. Then, identify the main idea and write two supporting details. Write them in the graphic organizer below.

Instrucciones: Lee el siguiente párrafo. Luego, identifica la idea principal y escribe dos detalles de soporte. Escríbelas en el organizador gráfico a continuación.

Comets are chunks of ice, dust, and rock that move through space. Some comets are *periodic*. This means that they make regular passes by Earth. Probably the most well-known periodic comet is called Halley's Comet. It can be observed from Earth every 75 years or so. Since 1600, people on Earth have seen this comet in the following years: 1607, 1682, 1759, 1835, 1910, and 1986. Halley's Comet is not expected to be seen again until the year 2061.

Main Idea

Supporting Detail

Supporting Detail

Invention Timeline

Directions: Use these clues to complete the timeline below. Some years are given. Use them—along with the clues and your math skills—to figure out the rest of the years.

Instrucciones: Usa estas claves para completar la siguiente línea de tiempo. Se dan algunos años. Úsalos—junto con las claves y tus habilidades matemáticas—para averiguar el resto de los años.

Invention Clues

- The first handheld calculator was developed 40 years after the first television image was transmitted.
- The first television image was transmitted just 2 years before sunglasses were invented.
- The World Wide Web was invented 60 years after the sunglasses were invented.
- Pre-sliced bread was introduced in 1928, and O-shaped oat cereal was introduced 13 years later.
- The first smartphones were developed 25 years after the first handheld calculators.

20th Century Inventions

Year	Invention
1927	the first television image transmitted
	pre-sliced bread introduced
	sunglasses invented
	O-shaped oat cereal introduced
1965	smoke detector for homes invented
	first handheld calculator
	World Wide Web invented
	first smartphone

A Tiring Tale

Directions: Read the following story. Use the Mini Dictionary to help you fill in the missing words.

Instrucciones: Lee el cuento siguiente. Usa el "Mini Dictionary" para que te ayude a completar las palabras faltantes.

Mini Dictionary

collapse—fall down

exhausted—very tired, fatigued

kayak—a small canoe

muscles—parts of the body that are used for movement and strength

navigate—ride around, sail

What a day! All of the ______(1)______ in my back and arms ache! I'm not moving from my bed for the rest of the week!

It started at 8:00 this morning—which is way too early if you ask me. It was my cousin's idea to take the ______(2)______ out on the lake behind our cabin. We must have been paddling around out there for hours in the hot sun. I was totally ______(3)______ by about 9:30, but we stayed out on the lake until almost noon. At one point, we had to ______(4)______ around a big pile of logs that were floating in the lake. That did me in. By the time we got home, I was ready to ______(5)______ on my bed and go to sleep.

Directions: On the blank, write the letter of the dictionary word next to the idea it best matches.

Instrucciones: En el espacio, escribe la letra de la palabra del diccionario próxima a la idea que combine mejor.

______	6. The bigger these are, the stronger a person is.	**a.** kayak
______	7. Use this to move down a stream.	**b.** collapse
______	8. Do this when you are tired.	**c.** navigate
______	9. Do this when you are moving around obstacles.	**d.** muscles
______	10. You feel this way when you've worked too hard.	**e.** exhausted

Breakfast Math

Directions: Use the Donut Price List to solve each word problem below. Tell how much each order cost and how much change each person received back. Use scratch paper to show your work.

Instrucciones: Usa la "Donut Price List" para resolver cada problema verbal. Di cuánto cuesta cada uno y cuanto cambio recibió cada persona. Use papel borrador para mostrar tu trabajo.

Donut Price List

Creamy Dream $1.99	Juicy Jelly $2.25	Round Mound $2.99	Tiger Twist $1.49

Order	Total Cost	Paid With	Change Back
1. 1 Juicy Jelly 1 Tiger Twist			
2. 1 Round Mound 1 Creamy Dream			
3. 2 Tiger Twists 1 Creamy Dream			
4. 2 Juicy Jellys 2 Creamy Dreams			
5. 2 Round Mounds 2 Juicy Jellys 1 Tiger Twist			

Then and Now

Directions: Gather information about yourself. Then, write the information in paragraph form.

Instrucciones: Reúne información sobre ti mismo. Luego, escribe la información en forma de párrafo.

My name is ____.

I was born in ____.

When I was a toddler, I used to play with _________________________

____

____.

These days, I like to play with ____________________________

____

____.

This year, I want to learn how to __________________________

____

____.

Some of my friends are _________________________________

____

____.

My favorite foods are __________________________________

____

____.

Some of my talents include ______________________________

____

____.

Life-Line

Born

Year 1

Year 2

Year 3

Year 4

Year 5

Year 6

Year 7

Year 8

Hidden Weather

Directions: Hidden in each sentence is a word that a meteorologist might use in a weather report. Each "weather word" can be found by combining the end of one word with the beginning of the next word(s). Underline the "weather word" in each sentence and write it on the line. Use the letter clues to help you. The first answer is written for you.

Instrucciones: Esconde en cada oración hay una palabra que un meteorólogo podría usar en un informe de clima. Cada "palabra meteorológica" se puede encontrar combinando el final de una palabra con el principio de la(s) siguiente(s) palabra(s). Subraya la "palabra meteorológica" en cada oración y escríbela en la línea. Utiliza las claves de letras para ayudarte. El ejemplo es para ti.

1. He i<u>s now</u> in fifth grade. (4 letters) snow
2. Mom made waffles this morning. (3 letters) __________
3. They had to move the show indoors. (4 letters) __________
4. Try this terrific yogurt! (3 letters) __________
5. I'd like to sail the seas on an inner tube! (6 letters) __________
6. She is unlikely to pass the test. (3 letters) __________
7. Which game is the best or most fun to play? (5 letters) __________
8. They found a box of rare coins in the attic. (4 letters) __________
9. Pack the camera in your suitcase. (4 letters) __________
10. We took the path under the bridge. (7 letters) __________
11. They played their music loudly all night. (5 letters) __________
12. The monster has torn a door off of its hinges. (7 letters) __________

The Birthday Equation

Directions: Did you know that there is an equation you can use to show the date of your birth? Try it out and see if it works. Follow the steps in order. Use the answer from the first step to complete the equation in the next step. Do this until every step has been completed.

Instrucciones: ¿Sabías que hay una ecuación que puedes usar para mostrar la fecha de tu nacimiento? Pruébela y ve si funciona. Sigue los pasos en orden. Utiliza la respuesta del primer paso para completa la ecuación en el siguiente paso. Haz esto hasta que hayas completado cada paso.

Steps	Equation	Answer
1. Add 18 to the number of your birth month. (For example, if you were born in February, you would add 2 + 18.)	________ + 18 = ________	
2. Take your answer from Step 1. Multiply it by 25.	________ × 25 = ________	
3. Take your answer from Step 2. Subtract 333 from it.	________ − 333 = ________	
4. Take your answer from Step 3. Multiply it by 8.		
5. Take your answer from Step 4. Subtract 554 from it.		
6. Take your answer from Step 5. Divide it by 2.		
7. Take your answer from Step 6. Add the day of your birth. (If you were born on May 12, you would add 12.)		
8. Take your answer from Step 7. Multiply it by 5.		
9. Take your answer from Step 8. Add 692 to it.		
10. Take your answer from Step 9. Multiply it by 20.		
11. Take your answer from Step 10. Add the last two digits of your birth year. (If you were born in 2011, then add 11.)		
12. Take your answer from Step 11. Subtract 32,940 from it.		

13. Follow these directions to write your answer in the box to the right.
    a. If you were born in October, November, or December, write the first two digits of your answer in the "a" spot. If you were born in any other month, write just the first digit of your answer in the "a" spot.
    b. Write the next two digits of your answer in the "b" spot.
    c. Write the final two digits of your answer in the "c" spot.

________ / ________ / ________
a b c

Home Run Decade

Directions: The double line graph below shows the number of home runs hit by the home run leader in the NL (National League) and AL (American League) in the decade of the 2010s. Use the graph to answer the questions below.

Instrucciones: El siguiente gráfico de doble línea muestra el número de jonrones conectados por el líder del jonrón en la NL (National League) y AL (American League) en la década del 2010. Utiliza la gráfica para responder las siguientes preguntas.

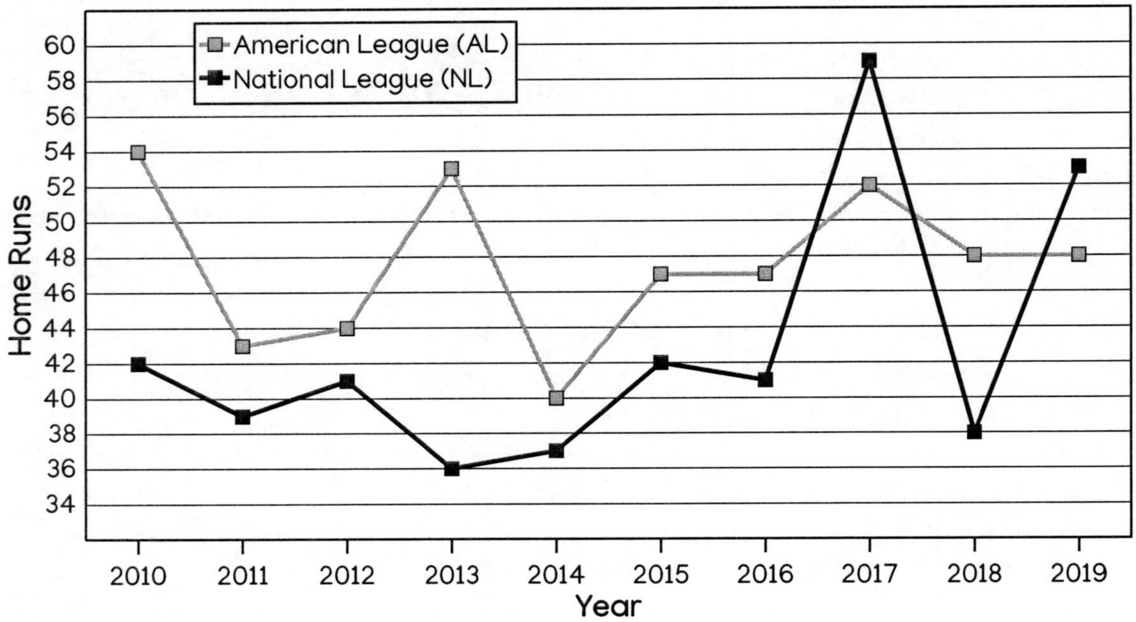

1. How many home runs did the AL leader hit in 2019? ____________________
2. How many home runs did the NL leader hit in 2016? ____________________
3. Find the highest home run total in the decade of the 2010s.
   a. How many home runs were hit? ____________________
   b. In what year was this total hit? ____________________
   c. In what league was this total hit? ____________________
4. Find the lowest home run total in the decade of the 2010s.
   a. How many home runs were hit? ____________________
   b. In what year was this total hit? ____________________
   c. In what league was this total hit? ____________________
5. In which two years did the NL leader hit more home runs than the AL leader?

____

The Clever Crow

Directions: Read the paragraph below. There are **15** errors that need to be corrected. Put proofreading marks where needed. Use this chart to help you:

Instrucciones: Lee el párrafo a continuación. Hay **15** errores que necesitan ser corregidos. Pon marcas de revisión donde sea necesario. Utiliza este cuadro para ayudarte a:

Proofreading Mark	Type of Error	Example	Number of Errors in Paragraph
⊙	Add a period.	That's the end⊙	4
?	Add a question mark.	Who is it?	1
≡	Make uppercase.	He is ralph.	7
/	Make lowercase.	I see a Tree.	3

A Crow named pete r Lee lived in st Louis, missouri. One tuesday in july, Pete wanted a drink of water. the only water was at the bottom of a pitcher, and Pete couldn't reach it How could Pete drink Pete picked up a little Pebble with his Beak and dropped it in the pitcher. Pete did this over and over until the water level was high enough for him to drink

Now It's Your Turn: Write 3–4 sentences about an animal doing something clever. Your story can be real or fictional. Make sure you proofread what you wrote.

Around and Around

What to Know

The **perimeter** is the distance around a geometric figure.

Directions: Compute the perimeter of each lawn in the problems below.

Instrucciones: Calcula el perímetro de cada césped en los siguientes problemas.

1. The Lawn Pros got a job edging a rectangular lawn that is 18 feet long and 10 feet wide. What is the perimeter of this lawn?

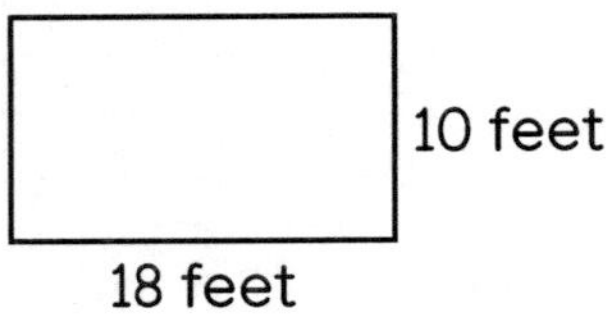

Answer: ____________________

2. One neighbor had a lawn shaped like a pentagon. Each side was 9 feet long. What is the perimeter?

Answer: ____________________

3. Mr. Cranky's lawn was shaped like a parallelogram. The shorter sides were 8 meters long each, and the longer sides were 22 meters long each. What is the perimeter?

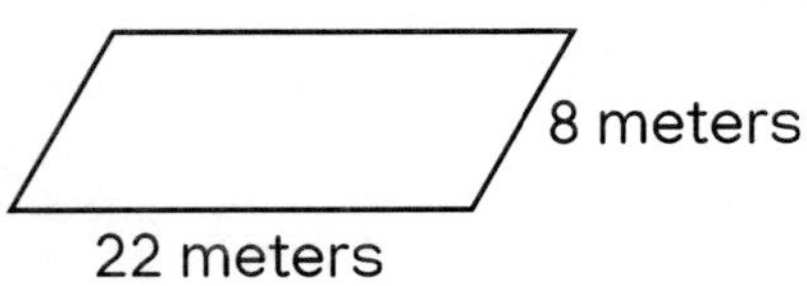

Answer: ____________________

4. Dr. Cutter's lawn was a trapezoid with these lengths: 9 meters, 12 meters, 11 meters, and 19 meters. What is the perimeter of his lawn?

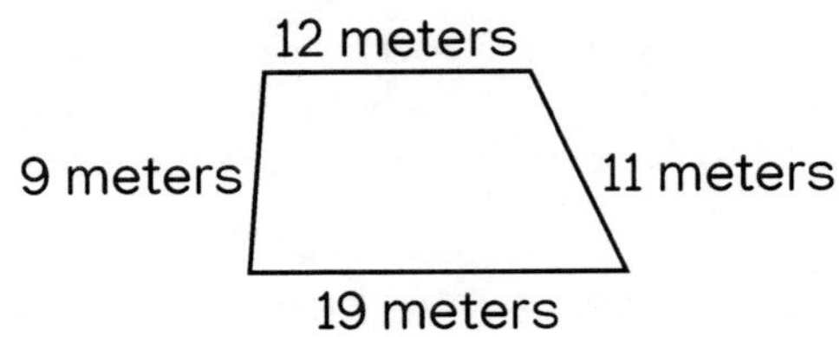

Answer: ____________________

5. One business had a lawn shaped like an isosceles triangle, with two sides that were 18 meters long and a base of 8 meters. What is the distance around this lawn?

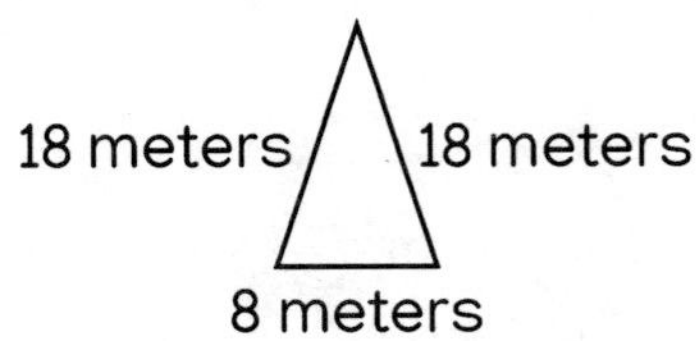

Answer: ____________________

6. The Grass Specialist edged a lawn with five sides. These were the lengths of each side: 9 meters, 7 meters, 6 meters, 12 meters, and 6 meters. What is the perimeter of this lawn?

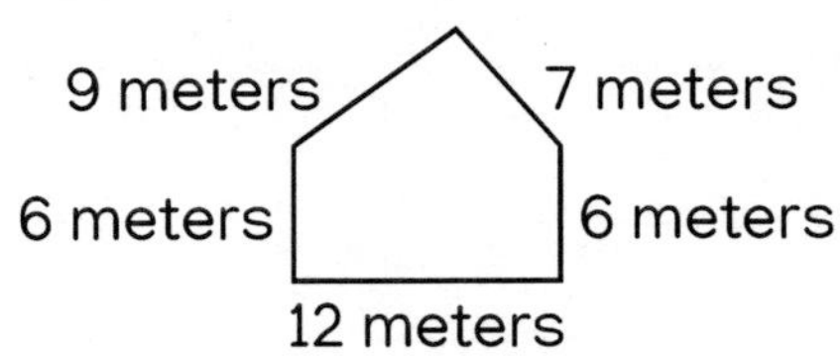

Answer: ____________________

Pluto's Journey

Directions: Read the two newspaper stories about two real events. Then number the events below in the order in which they happened in real life. (Note: Not all of the events listed below are directly mentioned in the stories.)

Instrucciones: Lee las dos historias del periódico sobre dos hechos reales. Luego menciona los eventos a continuación en el orden en que ocurrieron en la vida real. (Nota: No todos los eventos enumerados a continuación se mencionan directamente en las historias).

Tri-City Tribune **May 2, 1930**

Child Names Planet Pluto

The astronomers of Lowell Observatory have voted, and it is official: our solar system's newest planet will be named Pluto. This name was first suggested by Venetia Burney, an 11-year-old schoolgirl from Oxford, England. A fan of mythology, Ms. Burney believed that the planet should be named after Pluto, the Roman god of the cold, dark underworld.

Pluto's journey from discovery to named planet has been quick. It was first observed on February 18 of this year by Clyde Tombaugh at Lowell Observatory in Arizona. On March 24, a vote was held at Lowell Observatory to determine the planet's name. In addition to Pluto, the names Minerva and Cronus were also on the ballot. Yesterday, the results of the vote were announced, and they were unanimous. Every member chose Pluto for the planet's name.

Pluto now joins an exclusive club, as it becomes one of only nine planets in our solar system. Of these, Pluto is the farthest from the Sun. Astronomers believe that it is the coldest and smallest of the nine.

Tri-City Tribune **September 14, 2006**

Pluto Ousted!

Pluto has always been the little planet that was a little different than all the others. Yesterday, the International Astronomical Union (IAU) announced that Pluto will no longer be considered a planet. It will now be classified as a minor planet.

After a vote yesterday, the IAU has officially defined what it means to be a planet in our solar system, and Pluto does not meet all of the criteria. This decision is unpopular with some astronomers, while others believe Pluto should have been stripped of its planet status long ago.

In 1930, Pluto was named the ninth planet in our solar system, even though it is much smaller than the other eight planets and its orbit around the Sun follows a different path. With yesterday's ruling, Pluto now becomes just one of the nearly 400,000 minor planets that have been discovered.

____ The IAU announced that Pluto will no longer be considered a planet.

____ Clyde Tombaugh first observed Pluto.

____ Venetia Burney was born.

____ You were born.

____ At a vote held in Arizona, Pluto was given its name.

____ In 2007, the word *plutoed* was named Word of the Year. The word *plutoed* means "devalued."

Division Crossword

Directions: Solve each problem. Write each quotient as a number word in the number puzzle.

Instrucciones: Resuelve cada problema. Escribe cada cociente como una palabra numérica en el rompecabezas de números.

Across

1. 759 ÷ 69 = 11
4. 432 ÷ 72 = ______
5. 348 ÷ 29 = ______
7. 120 ÷ 10 = ______
8. 156 ÷ 52 = ______
10. 185 ÷ 37 = ______
12. 528 ÷ 66 = ______
13. 273 ÷ 21 = ______
14. 504 ÷ 72 = ______

Down

1. 209 ÷ 19 = ______
2. 297 ÷ 33 = ______
3. 510 ÷ 85 = ______
4. 546 ÷ 78 = ______
6. 484 ÷ 44 = ______
7. 360 ÷ 30 = ______
8. 110 ÷ 55 = ______
9. 980 ÷ 70 = ______
10. 480 ÷ 32 = ______
11. 244 ÷ 61 = ______
13. 270 ÷ 27 = ______

Story Boxes

Directions: Choose a list of words from one of the boxes below. Make up a story using all the words in the list in any order you want. Edit your story for punctuation, grammar, spelling, and language use.

Instrucciones: Elije una lista de palabras de uno de los cuadros a continuación. Inventa un cuento usando todas las palabras de la lista en el orden que desees. Revisa tu cuento en cuanto a puntuación, gramática, ortografía y el uso del lenguaje.

Box 1	Box 2	Box 3	Box 4
birthday party	ladybug	pizza	summer vacation
music	grassy field	Friday night	beach
invitations	tree	board games	sandcastle
balloons	ant hill	friends	towel
cake	sun	soda	sunscreen
family	picnic	ice cream	bathing suit

Food Fractions

Directions: Use the information in the recipe to help you solve the problems below. (*Hint:* Making a fraction of a recipe involves multiplication.)

Instrucciones: Usa la información de la receta de cocina para ayudarte a resolver los siguientes problemas. (*Sugerencia*: Hacer una fracción de una receta de cocina implica la multiplicación).

Red Hot Chili Recipe (Serves 20)

3 lbs. ground beef	4 oz. chili pepper
5 lbs. beans	6 oz. hot sauce
4 lbs. tomatoes	20 oz. tomato sauce
2 lbs. macaroni	16 oz. water

1. Mary wanted to make only $\frac{1}{4}$ of the recipe. How much did she need of each ingredient?

____________ lb. ground beef	____________ oz. chili pepper
____________ lbs. beans	____________ oz. hot sauce
____________ lb. tomatoes	____________ oz. tomato sauce
____________ lb. macaroni	____________ oz. water

2. Ray wanted to make only $\frac{1}{3}$ of the recipe. How much did he need of each ingredient?

____________ lb. ground beef	____________ oz. chili pepper
____________ lbs. beans	____________ oz. hot sauce
____________ lbs. tomatoes	____________ oz. tomato sauce
____________ lb. macaroni	____________ oz. water

3. Annette wanted to make only $\frac{1}{2}$ of the recipe. How much did she need of each ingredient?

____________ lbs. ground beef	____________ oz. chili pepper
____________ lbs. beans	____________ oz. hot sauce
____________ lbs. tomatoes	____________ oz. tomato sauce
____________ lb. macaroni	____________ oz. water

Green Thumb

Directions: Read the story, then circle the correct answers below.

Instrucciones: Lee el cuento, luego, haz un círculo alrededor de las respuestas correctas a continuación.

Kathryn had been working for hours in her grandmother's garden. It was a favorite pastime of hers. She loved the feel of the moist, warm dirt and the sound of the birds in the air. It had been a wonderful summer so far. Kathryn was anxious to see the fruits of her labor in the garden. She had planted all different types of flowers, and she was checking each day for a bloom from the green stalks poking their heads through the ground.

Things had not been easy for Kathryn. She had been fighting all summer. First, it was the soil. She had raked all of the rocks out of it and tirelessly removed any clods of dirt. She had added fertilizer and other additives to make the soil healthy and strong. Then, the slugs came along. Slugs and grubs were eating any plants and seeds she sowed. Finally, she fought the weather. After weeks of drought, the rains finally came, but then they wouldn't stop. Water had washed away the first crop of seeds. In despair, Kathryn stood outside dripping wet, setting up a net to prevent her soil from eroding. It worked temporarily.

Kathryn's grandmother took delight in Kathryn's hard work and diligence.

"It's going to pay off, dear," she encouraged Kathryn each time she arrived to work in the garden. "Your thumb is getting greener every day."

Kathryn always responded with the same comment, "My thumb doesn't look very green." Kathryn knew that she needed to be patient.

1. What would be a good title for this story?
   a. "Lost and Found in the Garden"
   b. "Hiring Scarecrows"
   c. "Work Before Play"
   d. "Gardening Is Hard Work"
2. What can you conclude about Kathryn after reading the passage?
   a. She is loved and adored by her friends.
   b. She is good at math.
   c. She is learning self-defense.
   d. She is hardworking.
3. Which sentence helps you answer the previous question?
   a. "It's going to pay off, dear," she encouraged Kathryn each time she arrived to work in the garden.
   b. Things had not been easy for Kathryn. She had been fighting all summer.
   c. Water had washed away the first crop of seeds.
   d. "My thumb doesn't look very green."

Favorite Meals

Directions: Read each clue to find out what each person eats and drinks. Use the chart below. If the answer is "yes," make a ✓ in the box. If the answer is "no," make an X in the box. Then, answer the statements below the chart.

Instrucciones: Lea cada clave para averiguar qué come y bebe cada persona. Utilice el gráfico. Si la respuesta es "sí", pon una ✓ en el recuadro. Si la respuesta es "no", marque la casilla con una X. Luego, contesta las afirmaciones debajo del cuadro.

Clues

- Tina likes to drink water when she has tacos for lunch.
- Jay never eats hot dogs, but he does like shakes.
- Marie always drinks soda when she eats pizza.

	Hamburgers	Pizza	Hot dogs	Tacos	Shakes	Soda	Water	Milk
Sean								
Jay								
Tina								
Marie								

1. Sean eats ______________________ and drinks ______________________.
2. Jay eats ______________________ and drinks ______________________.
3. Tina eats ______________________ and drinks ______________________.
4. Marie eats ______________________ and drinks ______________________.

Map Madness!

Do you see Peter? He is lost! Follow the cardinal directions (north, south, east, west) to get him back on track. Mark his ending spot with an X.

¿Ves a Pedro? ¡Está perdido! Sigue las direcciones cardinales (norte, sur, este, oeste) para ayudarle a volver al camino. Marca su punto final con una X.

Directions:

1. Go west on Third Ave.
2. Go south on Peach St.
3. Go east on First Ave.
4. Go north on Plum St.
5. Go east on Fifth Ave.
6. Go south on Pear St.
7. Go east on Second Ave.
8. Go north on Orange St.
9. Go west 4 blocks on Fourth Ave.
10. Go north 1 block.

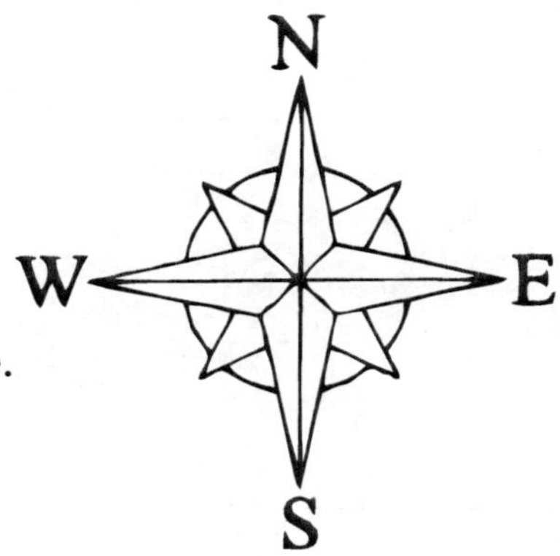

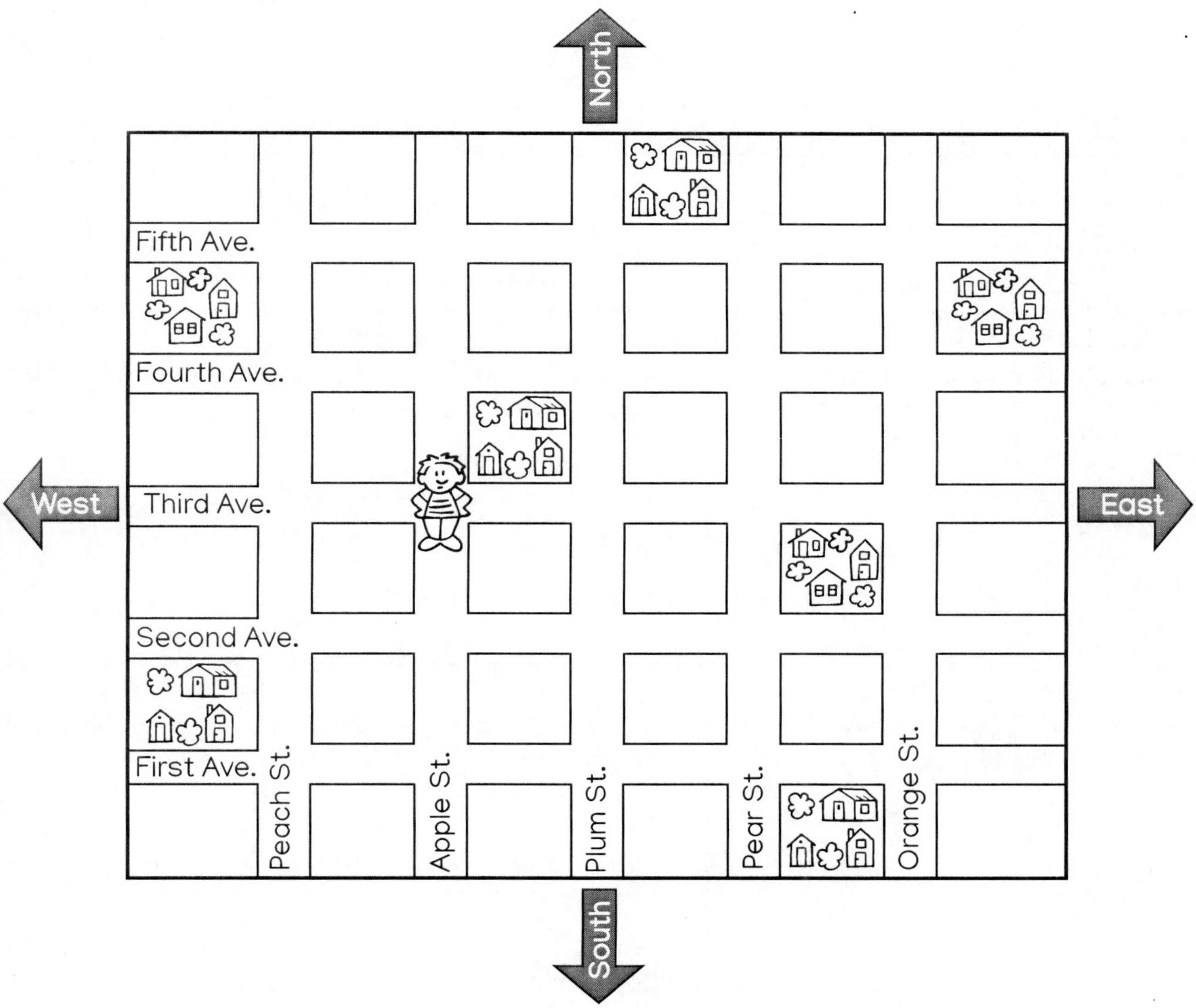

Mixed Math

Directions: Solve the problems. Show your work.

Instrucciones: Resuelve los problemas. Muestra tu trabajo.

1. Mr. Garcia bought a truck that cost $28,500. He will have 60 equal payments until the truck is paid off. How much will he pay each month? Select the correct operation below. Fill in the bubble beside the correct answer and then find out Mr. Garcia's monthly truck payment.

(A) Addition	(B) Subtraction	(C) Division	(D) Multiplication
$28,500 + 60	$28,500 − 60	60)$28,500	$28,500 × 60
$________	$________	$________	$________

2. $\frac{4}{6} \times \frac{1}{5} =$ ________

3. $\frac{2}{3} \times \frac{4}{5} =$ ________

4. $\frac{3}{4} \times \frac{1}{2} =$ ________

5. Each group of 4 students needs a bottle of glue and 6 sheets of construction paper for an art project. If there are 24 students in the class, how many sheets of paper will be needed altogether? How many bottles of glue will be needed?

________ sheets of paper and ________ bottles of glue

6. For a Valentine's Day gift, Robin received a box of chocolates from her husband. There were 54 pieces of candy in the box. Robin ate 6 pieces of candy. Write the fraction that represents how many candies are still in the box.

____

Madame Curie

Directions: Read the story, then circle the best answer to each question below.

Instrucciones: Lee el cuento, luego haz un círculo alrededor de la mejor respuesta a cada pregunta que figura a continuación.

Madame Curie, also known as Marie Curie, was a great scientist who made many important discoveries. Her story is one of inspiration and determination. She was born Maria Skłodowska on November 7, 1867, in Warsaw, Poland. Poland was in turmoil, and her family struggled to make ends meet. Maria's parents were teachers, and they taught their children the importance of school. Maria went on to graduate with honors from high school at sixteen years old. She lost her mother and her oldest sister to disease, and Maria struggled with a nervous illness. She went to the countryside to live with cousins.

Maria returned to Warsaw where she and her sister attended a "floating university." The classes were held at night, and they had to avoid being caught by the police. They eventually left for Paris where she received a degree in physics and math. It took many years, as she had to put her sister through school and then put herself through school.

Marie eventually married Pierre Curie. Madame Curie, along with her husband, discovered two radioactive elements. This work laid the foundation for future discoveries in nuclear physics and chemistry. She and her husband received the Nobel Prize for Physics. Madame Curie would go on to receive another Nobel Prize for Chemistry eight years later. Madame Curie was credited with making great strides in science.

1. Based on the reading passage, what interests did Marie have?
   - a. how to win the Nobel prize
   - b. how to run an experiment
   - c. math and chemistry
   - d. physics, chemistry, and math
2. Which is *not true* about Curie's experience with education?
   - a. She graduated high school with honors at age 16.
   - b. In Warsaw, she had to hide her attendance from the police.
   - c. She had to put her sister through school.
   - d. She struggled in her math classes and nearly failed.
3. What does the word *credited* mean as used in the third paragraph?
   - a. added to
   - b. known for
   - c. increasing debt
   - d. disregarded
4. What is the main idea of paragraph three?
   - a. Curie's discoveries and contributions to science
   - b. Curie's family background
   - c. Curie's love of science
   - d. Curie's choice of partner and husband

See the Pattern

Directions: Solve the problems.

Instrucciones: Resuelve los problemas.

1. Mary received $50.00 for her birthday. At the mall, she bought two books for $5.00 each, a new shirt for $15.00, and a movie for $17.99. Which number sentence is **NOT** a way to determine how much money Mary has left?

   a. $50 – $10 – $32.99 =

   b. $50 – $10 – $15 – $17.99 =

   c. $50 – $5 – $5 – $15 – $17.99 =

   d. $50 – $25 – $17.99 =

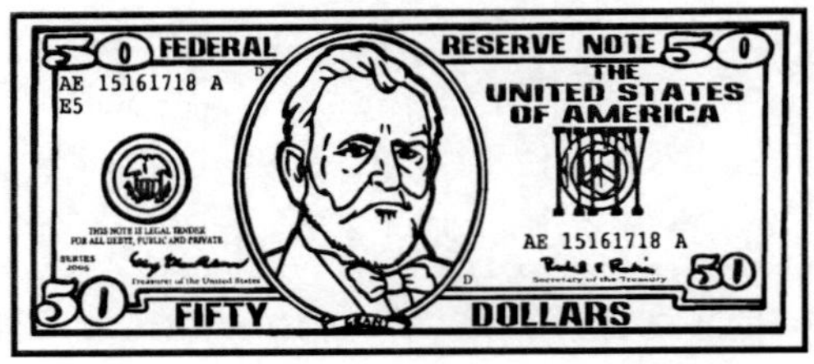

2. What is the rule for the pattern of numbers in the box on the right?

   a. Add 8, subtract 15

   b. Add 15, subtract 8

   c. Add 15, subtract 9

   d. Subtract 9, add 15

21, 36, 28, 43, 35

3. Wanda is on the swim team at school. Her coach keeps a log of the number of laps and the time it takes her to swim 100 meters. Each Friday, her coach gives her a copy of the log so she knows how well she did. Which statement correctly describes the table?

   a. Wanda swims three laps every four minutes.

   b. Wanda swims one lap every two minutes.

   c. Wanda swims seven laps every twenty-eight minutes.

   d. Wanda swims eight laps every six minutes.

Summer Log for Wanda

Days	Laps	Minutes
Monday	2	4
Tuesday	6	12
Wednesday	5	10
Thursday	5	10
Friday	10	20

4. Look at the pattern of numbers below. Write the two numbers that should go next in the pattern.

23, 31, 40, 50, 58, _____, _____

Diamante Poems

What to Know A **diamante poem** is in the shape of a diamond. A diamante poem is a descriptive poem.

Directions: Describe the events listed below.

Instrucciones: Describe los acontecimientos que se encuentra en la lista.

Event	Descriptive Words
First day of school	______________________
Learning to ride a bike	______________________
Having a slumber party	______________________
Getting a new pet	______________________
Family gathering	______________________
Sporting event	______________________

Directions: Write a diamante poem. Use one event listed above.

Instrucciones: Escribe un poema de siete versos sin rima. Usa un acontecimiento mencionado anteriormente.

____
(event being described)

__________ __________
(two words describing touch)

__________ __________ __________
(three words describing the tastes)

__________ __________ __________ __________
(four words describing the sounds)

__________ __________ __________
(three words describing the sights)

__________ __________
(two words describing the smells)

____
(adjective describing event)

Vehicles Sold

Directions: Make a horizontal bar graph showing the following information, then find the sums and the differences.

Instrucciones: Haz un gráfico de barras horizontales que muestre la siguiente información, luego encuentra las sumas y las diferencias.

	Sports Cars	61,917		Small Trucks	38,214
	Minivans	41,945		Big Trucks	43,127
	Station Wagons	73,958		SUVs	29,060
	Family Cars	62,000		Small Cars	54,498

Big Trucks														
Family Cars														
Small Cars														
Small Trucks														
Sports Cars														
Station Wagons														
SUVs														
Minivans														

10,000 20,000 30,000 40,000 50,000 60,000 70,000 80,000

1. Small Trucks + Big Trucks = ______________
2. Sports Cars + Small Cars = ______________
3. SUVs + Family Cars = ______________
4. SUVs + Minivans = ______________
5. Small Trucks – SUVs = ______________
6. Family Cars – Small Cars = ______________
7. Sports Cars – Big Trucks = ______________
8. Station Wagons – Minivans = ______________

The Best Definition

Directions: For each sentence below, choose the definition that matches the way the italicized word is used in the sentence. Circle the letter beside each correct answer.

Instrucciones: Para cada oración a continuación, elije la definición que combine con la forma en que la palabra que está en cursiva es utilizada en la oración. Haz un círculo alrededor de la letra junto a cada respuesta correcta.

1. After the mixture had been *heated* thoroughly, the chef added the cream.
   a. warmed, as in a vehicle or building
   b. intensified, as in an emotion
   c. warmed, as in a solid or liquid

2. The senator refused to let his staff pay for the expensive lunch *bill.*
   a. amount of money owed for a service
   b. the visor part of a cap
   c. text of a law presented for discussion

3. After watching videos all day, Tom's tablet was nearly out of *charge.*
   a. money expected for a service or good
   b. electrical power restored to a device
   c. guilt or blame placed for the committing of a crime

4. Someone had locked the gate, forcing us to *scale* the fence in order to leave.
   a. to climb up to or over the top of a tall object
   b. the relation between the real size of something and its size in a representation of it
   c. a flat plate-like part on a reptile, fish, or other animal

5. It was at that *point* that I decided this was my favorite movie ever.
   a. the sharp end of something
   b. a particular place or moment in time
   c. the main idea or reason for something

6. The new employee was asked to *file* the reports in alphabetical order.
   a. march in a line
   b. use a tool to smooth or reduce
   c. put something in a place where it can be retrieved at a later date

7. Sam sat against the *trunk* and snoozed in the shade beneath the leaves.
   a. a spacious compartment in a vehicle
   b. a sturdy box for holding things
   c. the main stem of a tree

8. I think we just broke the *record* for the fastest a pizza has ever been eaten.
   a. the highest or best accomplishment of something
   b. an account in writing intended to preserve information
   c. something on which sound has been stored so that it can be played back

Family Vacations

Directions: Make a horizontal bar graph showing the following information, then find the sums and the differences.

Instrucciones: Haz un gráfico de barras horizontales que muestre la siguiente información, luego encuentra las sumas y las diferencias.

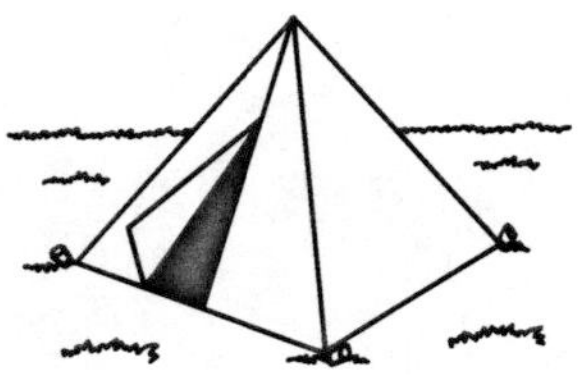

Beach 68,585	Camping 51,541
Road Trip 47,371	Big City 21,230
Mountains 32,371	Cruise 65,460
Stay Home 10,111	Another Country 16,221

Beach														
Road Trip														
Mountains														
Stay Home														
Camping														
Big City														
Cruise														
Another Country														

0 10,000 20,000 30,000 40,000 50,000 60,000 70,000

1. Beach + Stay Home = ________________
2. Mountains + Camping = ________________
3. Road Trip + Big City = ________________
4. Cruise + Another Country = ____________
5. Mountains – Stay Home = ____________
6. Road Trip – Mountains = ______________
7. Beach – Cruise = ____________________
8. Camping – Big City = ________________

Pros and Cons

Directions: Choose one of the topics below. Then, write three statements for it ("pros") and three arguments against it ("cons").

Instrucciones: Elije uno de los siguiente temas. Luego, escribe tres afirmaciones a favor ("pros") y tres argumentos en contra ("cons").

- The school week should only be four days long.
- No children should play contact sports such as football.
- Everyone should learn to ride a bicycle.
- Students should not watch television during the week.
- Winter school holidays should be longer and summer holidays shorter.

Pros

1. ______________________________

2. ______________________________

3. ______________________________

Cons

1. ______________________________

2. ______________________________

3. ______________________________

What's It Say?

Directions: Use the alphabet code to decode the message below.

Instrucciones: Usa el código alfabético para decodificar el siguiente mensaje.

A	=	26	J	=	17	S	=	8
B	=	25	K	=	16	T	=	7
C	=	24	L	=	15	U	=	6
D	=	23	M	=	14	V	=	5
E	=	22	N	=	13	W	=	4
F	=	21	O	=	12	X	=	3
G	=	20	P	=	11	Y	=	2
H	=	19	Q	=	10	Z	=	1
I	=	18	R	=	9			

___ ___ ___ ___   ___
14 26 16 22   26

___ ___ ___ ___ ___ ___ ___ ___ ___ ___
23 18 21 21 22 9 22 13 24 22

___ ___ ___ ___ ___ !
7 12 23 26 2

Directions: Now, decode this message. (*Challenge:* Can you do it without using the code?)

Instrucciones: Ahora, decodifique este mensaje. (Desafío: ¿Puedes hacerlo sin usar el código?)

___ ___ ___ ___ ___ ___   ___ ___ ___
15 18 8 7 22 13   26 13 23

___ ___ ___ ___ ___ .
15 22 26 9 13

Silly Sayings

Directions: Each box below contains a common saying. Study each box, then write the saying on the line. In the last box, try making one of your own!

Instrucciones: Cada cuadro a continuación contiene un dicho común. Estudia cada cuadro, luego escribe el dicho en la línea. En el último cuadro, ¡intenta crear uno propio!

BAN/ANA

1. ______________________________

HOROBOD

2. ______________________________

Rosie

3. ______________________________

stand

4. ______________________________

Once
___
a time

5. ______________________________

6. ______________________________

Number Crossword

Directions: Solve each problem. Write each answer in the puzzle. One is done for you.

Instrucciones: Resuelve cada problema. Escribe cada respuesta en el rompecabezas. Hay un ejemplo para ti.

Across

1. 942,977 – 861,165 = 81,812
4. 2,905,918 + 7,088,910 = ______
5. 336,073 + 400,368 = ______
6. 860,818 – 772,655 = ______
8. 448,231 + 114,474 = ______
10. 909,242 – 822,724 = ______
12. 730,598 – 693,107 = ______
14. 6,313,865 + 2,695,245 = ______
16. 1,650,039 – 1,224,916 = ______
18. 718,419 – 347,552 = ______
19. 5,947,045 + 3,795,684 = ______

Down

1. 6,419,280 – 5,601,491 = ______
2. 156,513 + 709,569 = ______
3. 2,086,126 + 2,877,237 = ______
7. 972,657 – 816,578 = ______
9. 2,683,045 + 5,083,865 = ______
11. 2,456,038 + 6,304,895 = ______
13. 8,184,722 – 7,995,005 = ______
15. 135,683 + 791,334 = ______
17. 6,542,311 – 6,213,935 = ______

Cause and Effect

Directions: Match each cause with its likely effect.

Instrucciones: Relaciona cada causa con su posible efecto.

1. ________ The car alarm went off.
2. ________ The lady drove very fast.
3. ________ He threw the watermelon.
4. ________ She gave the plant too much water.
5. ________ The electricity went out.

a. The policeman gave her a ticket.
b. The children ran away from the car.
c. The alarm clock didn't ring.
d. There was a puddle of water.
e. The watermelon split.

Directions: Write possible causes for the following effects.

Instrucciones: Escribe las causas posibles para los siguientes efectos.

6. ______________________________, so we left the movie theater early.
7. ______________________________, so I had to call my mom.
8. ______________________________, so our teacher gave us a pop quiz.
9. ______________________________, so I went to bed early.
10. ______________________________, so I finished my homework.

Directions: Write possible effects for the following causes.

Instrucciones: Escribe los efectos posibles para las causas a continuación.

11. I had a headache, so I ______________________________.
12. He forgot to study for his spelling test, so he ______________________________.
13. She won tickets to the circus, so she ______________________________.
14. My dog is too big, so I ______________________________.
15. I am allergic to peanuts, so I ______________________________.

Money Math Mystery

Directions: Solve the money problems below. Use the Letter Code Key to match each answer to the corresponding letter to solve this mystery:

Instrucciones: Resuelve los siguientes problemas de dinero. Use la "Letter Code Key" para relacionarla con cada respuesta correspondiente para resolver este misterio:

Why didn't the quarter roll down the hill with the nickel?

Letter Code Key

A = $54.39	H = $33.28	R = $73.92
B = $44.24	I = $19.92	S = $18.00
C = $37.17	M = $59.49	T = $55.56
D = $33.75	N = $80.96	U = $36.74
E = $14.64	O = $93.99	

		×
1.	$ 6.32	× 7
2.	$ 4.88	× 3
3.	$ 4.13	× 9
4.	$ 7.77	× 7
5.	$ 3.34	× 11
6.	$ 1.50	× 12
7.	$ 3.66	× 4
8.	$ 9.96	× 2
9.	$ 9.26	× 6
10.	$ 2.08	× 16
11.	$ 18.13	× 3
12.	$ 2.25	× 15
13.	$ 6.61	× 9
14.	$ 7.23	× 13
15.	$ 5.28	× 14
16.	$ 1.22	× 12
17.	$ 6.00	× 3
18.	$ 2.44	× 6
19.	$ 7.36	× 11
20.	$ 1.20	× 15
21.	$ 1.83	× 8

Coral Reef

Directions: Read the story, then circle the correct answers.

Instrucciones: Lee el cuento, luego haz un círculo alrededor de las respuestas correctas.

A coral reef is a beautiful underwater community filled with many different types of species. You can find fish, coral, sea plants, and much more. Coral reefs have been around for millions and millions of years. Recently, some scientists have started to believe that coral reefs may be in danger. Scientists believe that pollution and human **neglect** have destroyed more than a quarter of the world's coral reefs.

Some of the living animals that make up coral reefs are struggling to survive. For example, coral looks and feels like rock. This causes people to treat coral like rocks. But coral is actually made up of tiny, clear animals. These animals are called coral polyps. Coral sticks together to form large colonies. When coral polyps die, they leave a hard shell of limestone behind. Coral gets its color from tiny sea plants called algae. There is a delicate balance between algae and coral. Coral reefs provide homes and shelter for many sea animals and plants.

Pollution and bad fishing practices have caused harm to coral and algae. Another problem is the warming of the water. Algae cannot live in warmer waters, and therefore, coral loses its source of food and color. This process has been named coral bleaching.

Scientists are working hard to find solutions to the problems in coral reefs. Their goal is to protect and preserve this natural resource.

1. What is coral made up of?
   - a. sea anemone
   - b. tiny, clear animals
   - c. seaweed and moss
   - d. rocks and crevices

2. When coral polyps die, they leave a hard shell of
   - a. calcium.
   - b. helium.
   - c. carbon dioxide.
   - d. limestone.

3. What does the word *neglect* mean as used in the first paragraph?
   - a. respect
   - b. carelessness
   - c. love
   - d. attention

4. What is the main idea of this reading passage?
   - a. to inform the reader about the uniqueness of coral reefs and their need for protection
   - b. to inform the reader about how coral bleaching occurs
   - c. to explain the difference between the two different types of coral
   - d. to explain the life of marine biologists

Books Report

Directions: Look at the chart. It represents the reading and pledges of 15 students involved in the Read-a-Thon. After reading the chart, answer the questions.

Instrucciones: Mira el cuadro. El cuadro representa la lectura y compromisos de 15 alumnos que son parte del Read-a-Thon. Después de leer el cuadro, responde las preguntas.

Hudson Elementary School Read-a-Thon: Room 3			
Student Name	Total Books Read	Pledge per Book	Money Collected
Acevedo, Jennifer	31	10¢	$3.10
Adams, Joseph	5	10¢	$0.50
Barton, Michael	61	5¢	$3.05
Duran, Louis	17	15¢	$2.55
Edwards, Marylou	47	5¢	$2.35
Harrison, Trevor	11	25¢	$2.75
Lee, Rebecca	40	10¢	$4.00
Marshall, Barbara	9	50¢	$4.50
Peterson, David	102	5¢	$5.10
Ross, Kat	58	10¢	$5.80
Rublo, Anthony	83	5¢	$4.15
Tran, Alvin	14	10¢	$1.40
Yetter, Liz	75	5¢	$3.75
Total		—	

1. Which student read the most books? ______________________

2. What was the highest amount of money collected by one student? ______________

   Which student? ______________________

3. Who had the highest pledge of money per book? ______________________

4. Did the person who read the most books also collect the most money? ______________

5. Was the person who had the highest pledge of money per book the same person who collected the most money? ______________________

6. What was the total number of books read by all the students? ______________

7. How much money did the students earn for the library? ______________

List the Effects

Directions: List four possible effects for each event.

Instrucciones: Haz una lista de cuatro efectos posibles para cada acontecimiento.

Event #1 There was a half-an-hour wait to ride a roller coaster.

Possible Effect #1: ______________________________

____

Possible Effect #2: ______________________________

____

Event #2 The working conditions at a local construction site were unsafe.

Possible Effect #1: ______________________________

____

Possible Effect #2: ______________________________

____

Event #3 A pan of broccoli was left cooking on the stove, unattended.

Possible Effect #1: ______________________________

____

Possible Effect #2: ______________________________

____

Event #4 Dad's car keys fell behind the couch.

Possible Effect #1: ______________________________

____

Possible Effect #2: ______________________________

____

Event #5 Rain was forecast for the day of the class picnic.

Possible Effect #1: ______________________________

____

Possible Effect #2: ______________________________

____

Tally Table

Directions: The following table shows how 5th graders voted when asked to name their favorite game. Complete the table by filling in the Frequency column. Then answer the questions below.

Instrucciones: La siguiente tabla muestra cómo votaron los alumnos de quinto grado cuando se les pidió que nombraran a su juego favorito. Completa la tabla llenando la columna de "Frequency". Luego responde las preguntas a continuación.

Game	Card Game?	Tally	Frequency
Checkers	No	𝍸 𝍸 |||	13
Chess	No	𝍸 ||	
Twenty-One	Yes	||||	
War	Yes	𝍸 |||	
Hearts	Yes	||	
Old Maid	Yes	|	
Solitaire	Yes	||||	
none of the above		𝍸	

1. Which was the most favorite game? ____________________
2. Which was the least favorite game? ____________________
3. How many 5th graders didn't like any of these games? ____________________
4. How many more 5th graders preferred Chess to Old Maid? ____________________
5. How many 5th graders liked either Checkers or Chess? ____________________
6. How many more 5th graders preferred War to Solitaire? ____________________
7. How many 5th graders chose a card game as their favorite? ____________________
8. How many total students participated in the survey? ____________________

What Happened Next?

What to Know

When you write about something that happened to you or something that you do, it must be in the right time order. Another name for this is chronology. The things you write about in a paragraph should usually be in chronological (or time) order to make sense.

Directions: Put the events below in chronological order by ordering them from first (1) to last (5). The first one has been done for you.

Instrucciones: Pon los siguientes eventos en orden cronológico ordenándolos desde el primero (1) hasta el último (5). El ejemplo es para ti.

A. __2__ eat breakfast
__1__ wake up
__5__ go to school
__4__ go out the door
__3__ brush teeth

B. _____ bait a hook
_____ clean a fish
_____ eat a fish
_____ catch a fish
_____ cook a fish

C. _____ mail the letter
_____ put the letter in an envelope
_____ write a letter
_____ wait for an answer
_____ seal the envelope

D. _____ type a book report
_____ click on word processing
_____ turn on the printer
_____ turn on the computer
_____ print the book report

E. _____ put anti-itch ointment on arm
_____ wash the bite area
_____ feel a bite, "Ouch!"
_____ hear a buzz
_____ scratch the bump

F. _____ buy popcorn
_____ leave the theater
_____ stand in the ticket line
_____ buy a ticket
_____ watch a movie

G. _____ find an old Halloween mask
_____ clean up your room
_____ sneak up on your brother
_____ put it on
_____ jump out at him

H. _____ snap on the leash
_____ guide your dog back home
_____ get the leash
_____ whistle for your dog
_____ walk your dog

ABC Puzzlers

Directions: Determine the hidden meaning of each clue. Each initial below represents a key word. Find the missing words. The first one has been done for you.

Instrucciones: Determinar el significado oculto de cada pista. Cada inicial representa una clave palabra. Encuentra las palabras que faltan. El primero ha sido hecho por ti.

1. 8 P in the SS 8 planets in the solar system	5. 4 Q in a D
2. 26 L in the A	6. 7 C on planet E
3. 52 W in a Y	7. At 32 D, water F
4. TE invented the LB	8. GW was the first P

Hidden Animals

Directions: Hidden in each sentence is the name of an animal. Each can be found by combining the end of one word with the beginning of the next word(s). Underline the animal name in each sentence and write the animal name on the line. Use the letter clues to help you. The first answer has been written for you.

Instrucciones: Escondido en cada oración está el nombre de un animal. Cada uno se puede encontrar combinando el final de una palabra con el comienzo de la(s) palabra(s) siguiente(s). Subraya el nombre del animal en cada oración y escribe el nombre del animal en la línea. Usa las claves de las letras para ayudarte. El ejemplo es para ti.

1. To and fro go the holiday shoppers in the mall. (4 letters) frog
2. Half the people came late to the party. (5 letters) ________
3. They do good work when they try their best. (3 letters) ________
4. I can go at 6:30 tomorrow morning. (4 letters) ________
5. Steffi should be pleased with the results. (4 letters) ________
6. He ran a slow lap around the track. (3 letters) ________
7. Please allow me to help you with that. (4 letters) ________
8. We will leave for the picnic at noon. (3 letters) ________
9. I will be around here if you need me. (4 letters) ________
10. The teacher made Ernie stay home. (4 letters) ________
11. Will I only need to pack one pair of shoes? (4 letters) ________
12. This path ends here. (3 letters) ________
13. Aren't these toys terrific? (6 letters) ________
14. I am either sixth or seventh in line. (5 letters) ________
15. They ship pots and pans right to your home. (5 letters) ________

Sports Pictograph

Directions: This pictograph represents a survey of sports preferences among grade-school students in the 4th through 6th grades. Study the pictograph and answer the questions below.

Instrucciones: Este pictograma representa una encuesta sobre las preferencias deportivas entre estudiantes de la escuela primaria que se encuentran en 4to a 6to grado. Estudia el pictograma y contesta las siguientes preguntas.

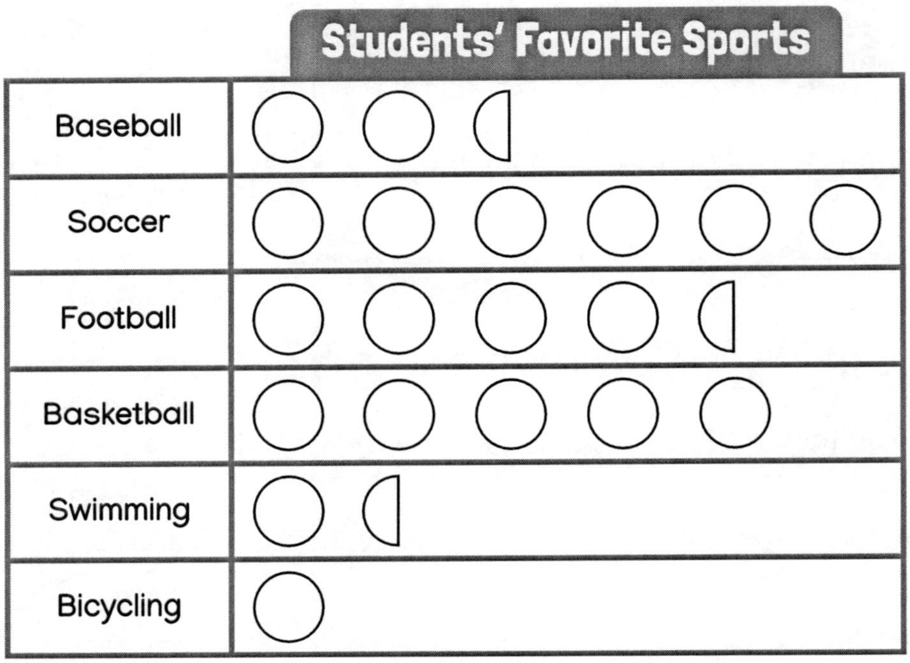

Key = ○ = 10 students

1. How many students prefer to play basketball? ________________
2. How many students prefer bicycling as their favorite sport? ________________
3. How many students prefer to play baseball? ________________
4. How many students prefer football as their favorite sport? ________________
5. Which are the two most favorite sports? ____
6. Which are the two least favorite sports? ____
7. How many more students prefer soccer to swimming? ________________
8. How many more students prefer football to baseball? ________________

Electricity

Directions: Read the story, then circle the correct answers.

Instrucciones: Lee el cuento, luego haz un círculo alrededor de las respuestas correctas.

We use electricity every day. We use it to light rooms, dry clothes, and toast bread. We need it for our computers and TVs. There are times that we need more electricity than can be made. All electricity gets generated in a power plant. When we try to use more electricity than the plant can produce at one time, we have blackouts. The power goes off completely.

Wires carry electricity from power plants to your home. Some things, like copper, let electricity flow through them. These are called conductors. Electric wires are copper. Other things, like rubber, stop electricity. Power does not pass through them. These are called insulators. Copper wires have rubber covers to keep the electricity from leaving the wire.

Lightning is natural electricity. A single lightning bolt has **tremendous** power. It could light up a city for one year. Scientists want to find a way to tap into this natural energy source.

1. What is a machine that would still work during a power outage (blackout)?
   - a. an air conditioner
   - b. a battery-powered radio
   - c. a refrigerator
   - d. a television

2. Why would a large demand for electricity cause a blackout?
   - a. People can't pay enough money to get the amount of electricity they need.
   - b. A high demand for power creates an explosion at a power plant.
   - c. When the power plant is overwhelmed by demand, it shuts down.
   - d. When the power plant is overwhelmed by demand, it starts using lightning for power.

3. Of the following choices, which would make a good insulator?
   - a. rubber boots
   - b. a metal pan
   - c. a lightning rod
   - d. copper wires

4. What does the word *tremendous* mean as used in the third paragraph?
   - a. very little
   - b. surprising
   - c. enormous
   - d. tiny

City Grid

Directions: Study the city grid. Notice where landmarks, such as the bank and park, are located. Notice which numbers are positive and which are negative. Note how the four quadrants are labeled: I, II, III, and IV. Use the information to answer the questions below. Always go across before going up or down, then use the point for finding the coordinate.

Instrucciones: Estudia la cuadrícula de la ciudad. Fíjate dónde se encuentran los puntos de referencia, tales como el banco y el parque. Fíjate qué números son positivos y cuáles son negativos. Ten en cuenta cómo están etiquetados los cuadrantes: I, II, III y IV. Usa la información para responder las siguientes preguntas. Cruce siempre antes de subir o bajar, luego usa el punto para encontrar la coordenada.

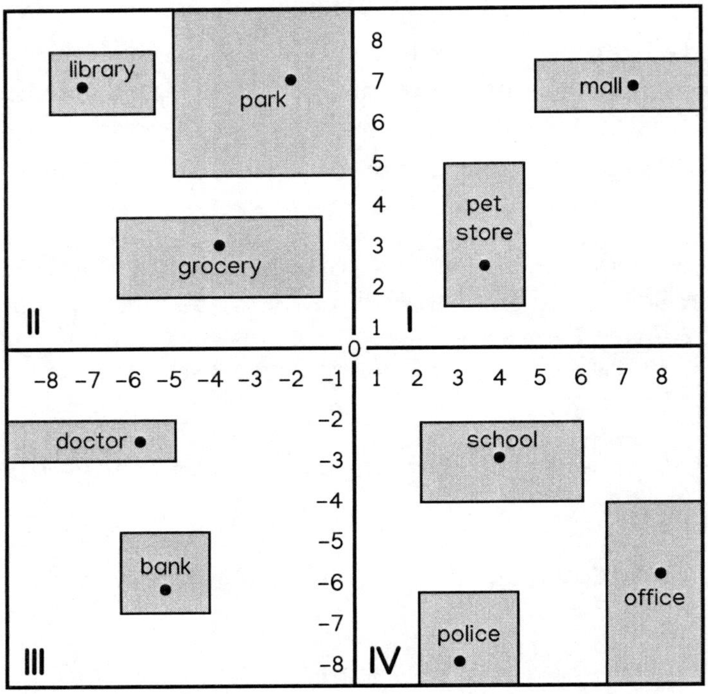

1. What feature is located at coordinate (7, 7)? ____________________
2. What building is located at coordinate (4, –3)? ____________________
3. What business is located at coordinate (–5, –6)? ____________________
4. Which quadrant has only negative coordinates? ____________________
5. Which quadrant has only positive coordinates? ____________________
6. What coordinate is shown in the police station? ____________________
7. What building is located at coordinate (–7, 7)? ____________________
8. What feature is located at coordinate (–2, 7)? ____________________

Join Sentences

What to Know

Two simple sentences, joined together, make a **compound sentence. Conjunctions** help to combine simple sentences. Words such as *and* and *but* are conjunctions.

Example: I bought apples, and Matt bought figs.
Tom likes pears, but his sister likes plums.

Directions: Use *and*, *but*, or *so* to join the two sentences.

Instrucciones: Utiliza *y*, *pero* o *entonces* par combinar las dos oraciones.

and but so

1. I am hungry, ____________ I will eat lunch.
2. He wanted to go, ____________ his dad wouldn't let him.
3. She called his name, ____________ he didn't hear her.
4. Pia likes jelly beans, ____________ she likes chocolate candy.
5. There's enough room in our car, ____________ you can come with us.

Directions: Add your own sentence to make a compound sentence.

Instrucciones: Agrega tu propia oración para hacer una oración compuesta.

6. Jack played tennis, and ____.
7. I eat lettuce, but ____.
8. Saul wanted a pet bird, so ____.

Directions: Join two sentences with a conjunction by drawing lines.

Instrucciones: Combina dos oraciones con una conjunción dibujando líneas.

9. Tom wants to go in the pool,	and	you may go home.
10. Mia has black hair,		the pool is full.
11. The bell has rung,	so	I also like tea.
12. Greg knocked on the door,		he can't swim.
13. I like coffee,	but	Ann has red hair.
14. It rained heavily,		no one answered.

Area Math

Formulas

Area of a rectangle = length × width
Area of a parallelogram = base × height
Area of a triangle = base × height ÷ 2

Directions: Use the formulas to compute the area of each lawn in the problems below.

Instrucciones: Usa las fórmulas para calcular el área de cada césped en los problema a continuación.

1. Mr. Steven's yard is a parallelogram that is 9 feet high and 15 feet at the base. What is the area of his lawn?

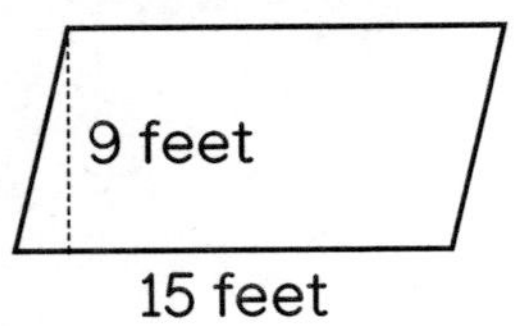

Answer: ____________________

2. Mrs. Frank's rectangular lawn measures 14 feet by 7 feet. What is the area of her lawn?

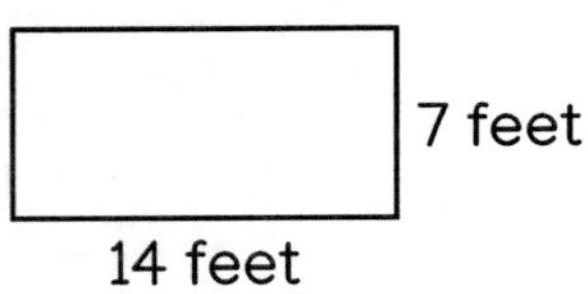

Answer: ____________________

3. Mr. Ellis's lawn is shaped like an isosceles triangle. It has a height of 8 feet and a base of 6 feet. What is the area of his lawn?

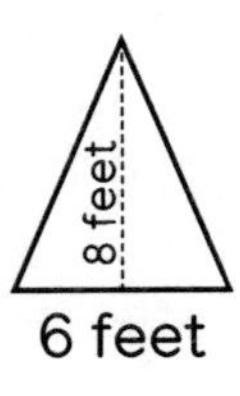

Answer: ____________________

4. Mr. Sharp's lawn is a triangle wih a height of 16 feet and a base of 13 feet. What is the area of his lawn?

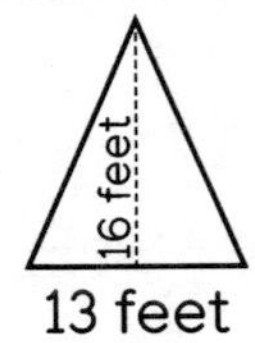

Answer: ____________________

5. The Lawn Magician mowed their next-door neighbor's rectangular lawn which was 8 feet by 24 feet. What was the area of the lawn?

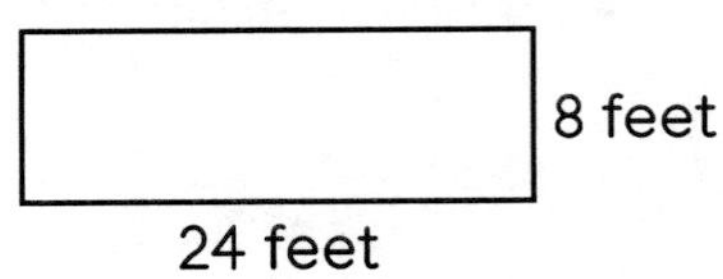

Answer: ____________________

6. Mrs. Potter's lawn is a parallelogram that is 8 feet high and 9 feet at the base. What is the area of her lawn?

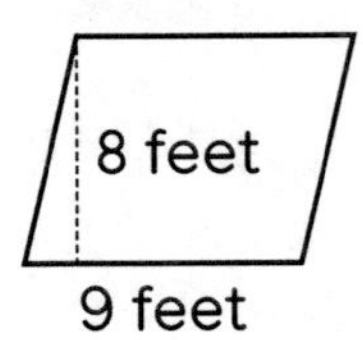

Answer: ____________________

Same Sound

What to Know

Homophones are two or more words that sound the same have different meanings and different spellings.

Directions: Select the correct homophone from the parentheses to fill in the blank(s) in each sentence.

Instrucciones: Selecciona el homófono correcto de entre los paréntesis para completar los espacios en blanco en cada oración.

1. A rectangle has ____________________ sides.
   (for/four)

2. To watch his sister Jane lose the race was more than John could ____________________.
   (bear/bare)

3. How many times have you ____________________ the doughnut shop without stopping?
   (passed/past)

4. Mother said, "Go to bed because __________ too late for you to be up on a school night."
   (its/it's)

5. "____________________ going to clean this up?" Dad asked about the spilled milk.
   (Who's/Whose)

6. The drum major ____________________ the band in the parade.
   (led/lead)

7. Do you think that the world will ever be completely at ____________________?
   (peace/piece)

8. The Wilson twins learned how to button ____________________ shirts when they were only
   (their/there/they're)
   ____________________ years old.
   (to/too/two)

9. I do not think it is ________________ that my brother would not loan me bus____________.
   (fair/fare) (fair/fare)

10. My editor does not think it is ____________________ that the judge will not allow me to
    (right/rite/write)
    ____________________ a newspaper story about the mysterious ____________________
    (right/rite/write) (right/rite/write)
    in which the barbarians participated.

Real-World Geometry

Directions: Answer the following questions. Circle the correct answer or fill in the blanks.

Instrucciones: Responde las siguientes preguntas. Haz un círculo alrededor de cada respuesta correcta o completa los espacios en blanco.

1. Which street is perpendicular to Sam St.?

   a. Pete

   b. Jody

   c. Kyle

   d. Gordon

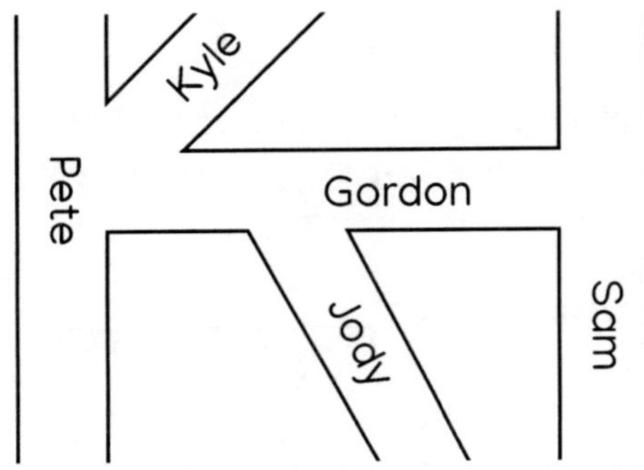

2. David worked on his racecar from 5:30 p.m. to 6:15 p.m. on Monday, from 6:10 p.m. to 7:00 p.m. on Tuesday, from 2:25 p.m. to 3:40 p.m. on Wednesday, and from 1:20 p.m. to 2:10 p.m. on Thursday. How many total minutes did David work on his car during the four-day period? Fill in the table to show your answer.

Day	Monday	Tuesday	Wednesday	Thursday	Total Minutes
Minutes					

3. Lee is buying a car cover for his son's car. The length of the car is 14 feet. He can buy the car cover in lengths of 96 inches for $21.50, 144 inches for $28.90, 180 inches for $32.60, and 240 inches for $38.75. Lee wants the car cover to fit snugly and to spend the least amount of money possible. Which car cover would be the most reasonable buy for Lee to make?

   a. 96 inches　　b. 144 inches　　c. 180 inches　　d. 240 inches

4. What statement about the shape below is **true**?

   a. Side **MN** and side **QP** are parallel.

   b. There are no parallel sides on the shape.

   c. Side **QP** and side **NO** are parallel.

   d. Side **MQ** is perpendicular to side **QP**.

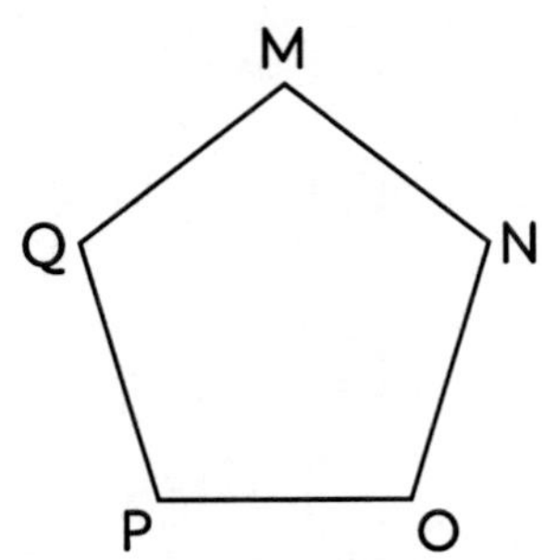

Fact or Opinion?

What to Know

Many sentences are statements. A statement begins with a capital letter and ends with a period.

Example: I like apples.
Mary sings pop songs.

Directions: Write a statement about each picture.

Instrucciones: Escribe una afirmación para cada una de las fotos.

1.

2.

3.

4.

Directions: Decide if these sentences are *facts* (true) or *opinions* (what someone thinks is true). Then, write **fact** or **opinion** on the lines.

Instrucciones: Decide si estas oraciones representan *facts* (verdaderas) u *opinions* (lo que alguien piensa que es verdad). Luego, escribe **fact** u **opinion** en las líneas.

5. Sacramento is the capital of California. ____________
6. Water boils at 100 degrees Celsius. ____________
7. The koala is Australia's favorite native animal. ____________
8. Eating an apple a day will keep you healthy. ____________

Directions: Write one fact and one opinion about one of the pictures above.

Instrucciones: Escribe un hecho y una opinión acerca de una de las siguientes fotos.

9. ____________

10. ____________

Droodles

What to Know

Droodles are artistic interpretations of brainteasers. Pictures or illustrations are used to present information. Symbols may represent different things depending on the context. Word clues may be added.

Directions: What could these droodles be? Write your answers on the lines. The first one has been done for you.

Instrucciones: ¿Qué podrían ser estos garabatos? Escribe tus respuestas en las líneas. El ejemplo es para ti.

Droodle #1

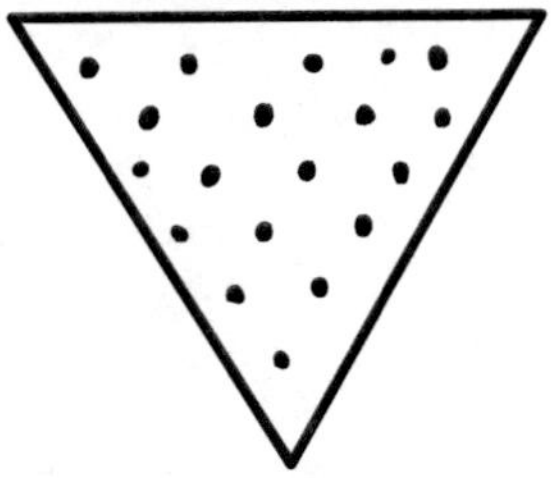

What could it be? a slice of cheese pizza topped with sausage bits

Droodle #2

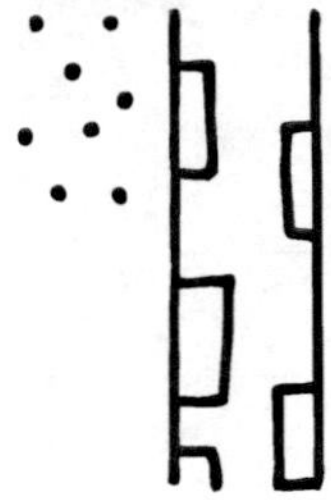

What could it be? ______________________

Droodle #3

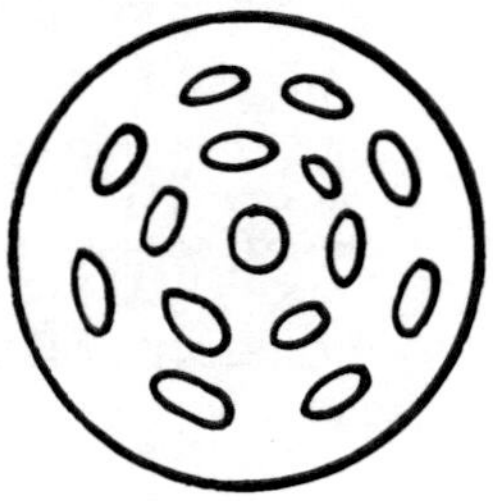

What could it be? ______________________

Droodle #4

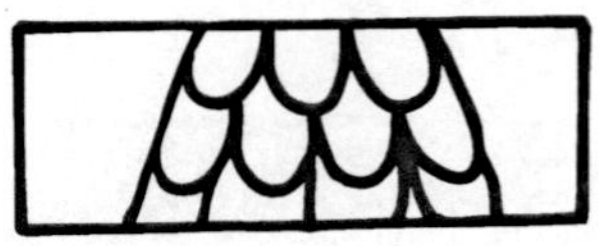

What could it be? ______________________

Droodle #5

What could it be? ______________________

Droodle #6

What could it be? ______________________

If True, Then Do

Directions: To solve the puzzle and find the hidden word, read the sentences below. If the statement is true, then color the numbered puzzle spaces as directed.

Instrucciones: Para resolver el rompecabezas y encontrar la palabra escondida, lee las siguientes oraciones. Si la declaración es verdadera, colorea los espacios numerados del rompecabezas tal como se indica.

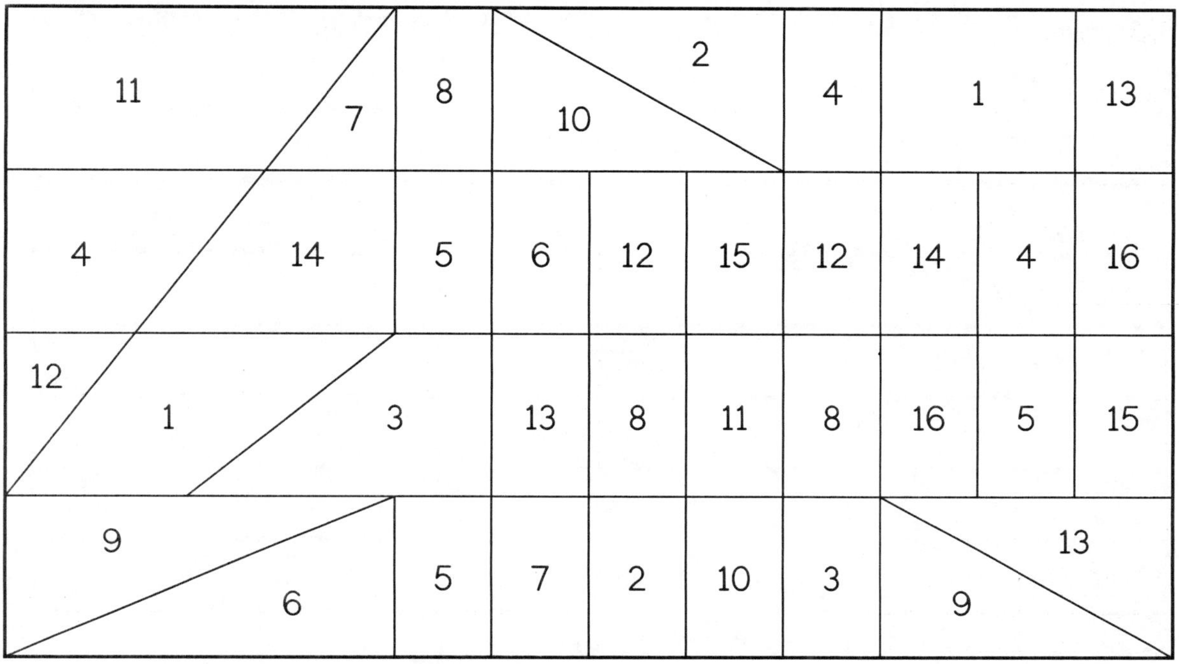

- If cows give milk, color the #1 spaces.
- If whales swim, color the #2 spaces.
- If birds have scales, color the #3 spaces.
- If worms have feet, color the #4 spaces.
- If lions have stripes, color the #5 spaces.
- If camels have humps, color the #6 spaces.
- If pigs "oink," color the #7 spaces.
- If snakes are mammals, color the #8 spaces.
- If squirrels eat nuts, color the #9 spaces.
- If elephants have trunks, color the #10 spaces.
- If zebras have stripes, color the #11 spaces.
- If chickens "quack," color the #12 spaces.
- If spiders spin webs, color the #13 spaces.
- If cats have fur, color the #14 spaces.
- If ants are insects, color the #15 spaces.
- If eagles have feathers, color the #16 spaces.

What word did you color? ______________________________

Family Budget

Directions: The following table shows the budget that a family must follow. Calculate the yearly amount of their budget below. Then, answer the questions that follow.

Instrucciones: La siguiente tabla muestra el presupuesto que debe seguir una familia. Calcular la cantidad anual de su presupuesto. Luego, responde las preguntas que siguen.

Monthly Billing Item	Monthly Amount	Yearly Amount
Home	$1,522.45	
Cable TV	$75.40	
Electricity	$120.34	
Gas	$60.52	
Telephone	$68.95	
Cars	$650.39	
Food	$200.85	
Clothing	$102.09	
	Total Yearly Expenditures	

1. Now that the family knows their yearly expenses, they need to plan for their savings. If they save $45.50 a month, how much will they have saved by the end of the year?

2. They would like to cut one bill in half. If they cancel everything but basic service, their cable TV bill will be reduced to half of what they currently pay. How much would they pay for basic service each month?

3. What would be the new yearly bill for basic service of cable TV?

4. What is the combined amount this family pays for electricity and gas each year?

5. How much more does this family spend on food than on clothing each year?

Let's Begin

What to Know

A **capital letter** is used for the first letter of a sentence, the first letter in proper nouns, and the pronoun *I*.

Directions: Color the boxes with words that should begin with capital letters.

Instrucciones: Colorea los recuadros con palabras que deben comenzar con mayúsculas.

asia	england	murray river	south	uranus
insects	kansas city	october	stranger	vietnam
canada	london	pacific ocean	summer	wattle street
christmas	michelle	plate	swan lake	wednesday
easter	mount everest	shamrock hotel	tables	white house

Directions: Complete the sentences.

Instrucciones: Completa las oraciones.

1. My full name is ______________________________.
2. My birthday is in the month of ______________________________.
3. The street I live on is ______________________________.
4. The school I attend is ______________________________.
5. My teacher's name is ______________________________.
6. I live in the town or city of ______________________________.
7. The country I would most like to visit is ______________________________.

Directions: Rewrite the following sentences correctly.

Instrucciones: Vuelve a escribir las oraciones en forma correcta.

8. last saturday, julie went to chicago

____

9. at christmas, we are going to italy, which is a country in europe

____

10. the wedding will take place at st patrick's church in greensboro

____

Monthly Math

Directions: Margo is about to rent her first apartment. She has estimated that she can spend up to $7,800 a year for the monthly rent. The following problems describe the things that she must consider when trying to decide which apartment will be the best for her.

Instrucciones: Margo está a punto de alquilar su primer apartamento. Ha estimado que puede gastar hasta $7,800 al año por el alquiler mensual. Los siguientes problemas describen las cosas que ella debe tener en cuenta al tratar de decidir qué apartamento será el mejor para ella.

1. Margo looked at Apartment A. It was a two-bedroom apartment that costs $700 a month.

   a. What is the yearly amount for the rent? ____________

   b. Based on her budget, can she afford to live there? ____________

2. Margo saw Apartment B. The rent was $680 a month. The landlord said that she could share the apartment with a friend. They would each pay an equal amount of the rent.

   a. What would she have to pay for rent by the end of the year? ____________

   b. Could Margo afford this apartment if she shared it? ____________

3. Margo found Apartment C near her job. It cost $625.55 a month. It was a large space with two full baths and two bedrooms. She really liked it.

   a. What is the yearly amount of rent for this apartment? ____________

   b. Can she afford this place? ____________

4. Which two apartments described above can Margo afford? ____________

   By the end of the first year, how much more would she have paid for the more expensive of these two apartments? ____________

Tiny Words

What to Know The prefixes *micro–* and *mini–* mean "tiny."

Example: *Microsurgery* means "delicate surgery done under a microscope."
Minuscule means "very tiny."

Directions: Write the correct word beneath its picture. The first one has been done for you.

Instrucciones: Escribe la palabra correcta debajo de cada foto. El ejemplo es para ti.

~~microphone~~ mini terrier microscope minibus microwave minivan

1.	2.	3.
 microphone	 ______	 ______
4.	5.	6.
 ______	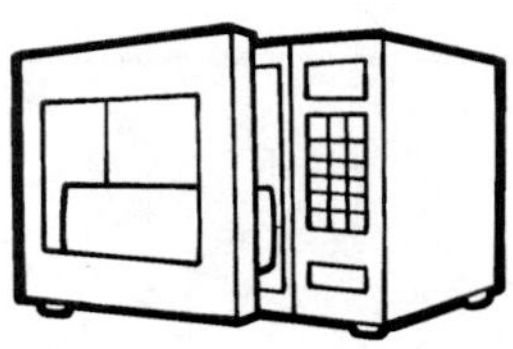 ______	 ______

Directions: Circle the name of the item that's smaller.

Instrucciones: Haz un círculo alrededor del artículo que sea más pequeño.

7.	maximum	(minimum)	11.	minute	hour
8.	miniskirt	skirt	12.	telescope	microscope
9.	microfilm	film	13.	raindrop	microbe
10.	megaphone	microphone	14.	mini terrier	St. Bernard

How Many Degrees?

Directions: Compute the number of degrees in each unmarked angle. Remember, the interior angles of a quadrilateral always add up to 360°.

Instrucciones: Calcula el número de grados en cada ángulo que no esté marcado. Recuerda, los ángulos interiores de un cuadrilátero siempre suman 360°.

1.

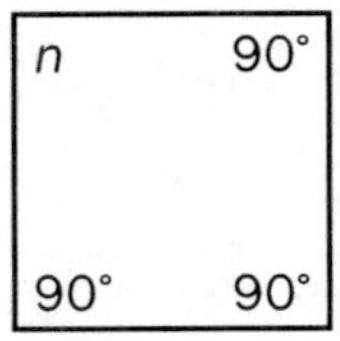

$n =$ ________

2.

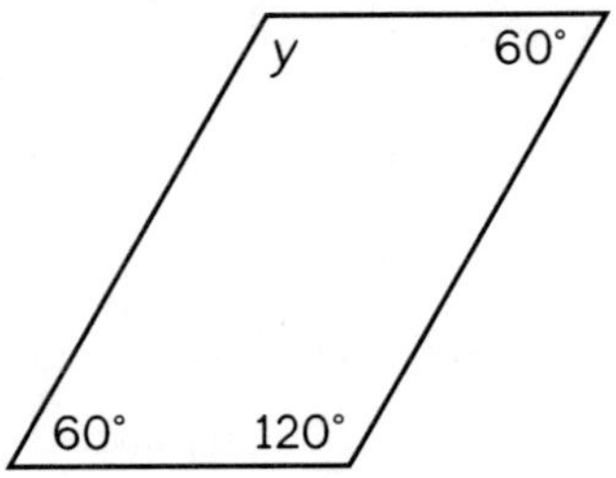

$y =$ ________

3.

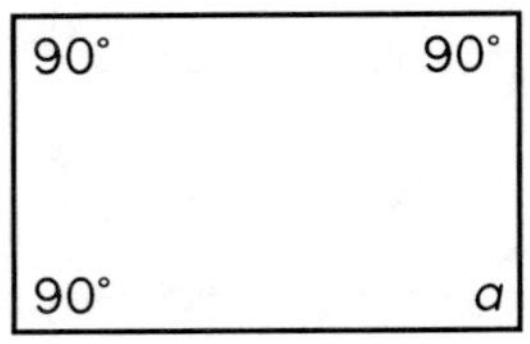

$a =$ ________

4.

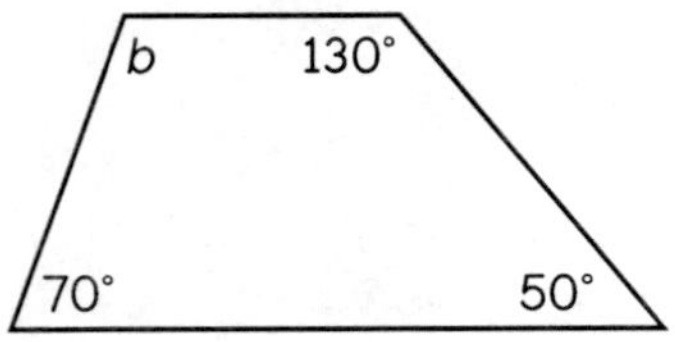

$b =$ ________

5.

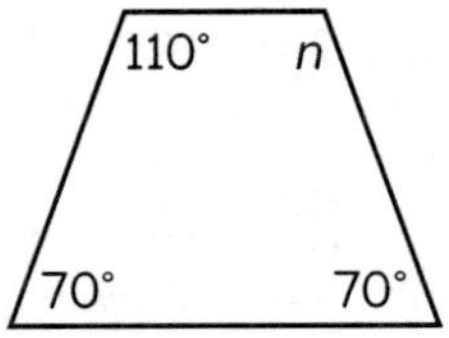

$n =$ ________

6.

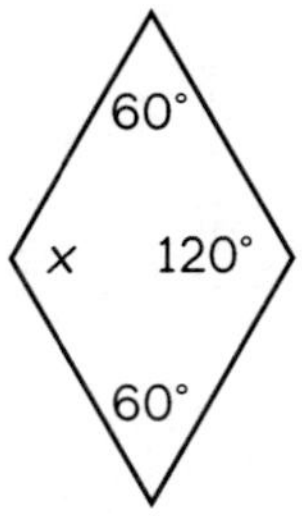

$x =$ ________

7.

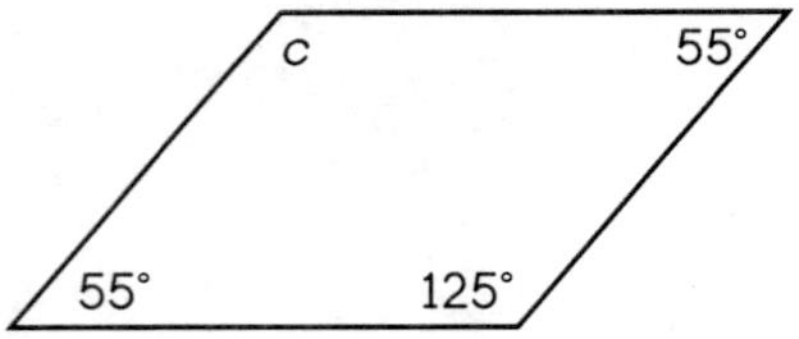

$c =$ ________

8.

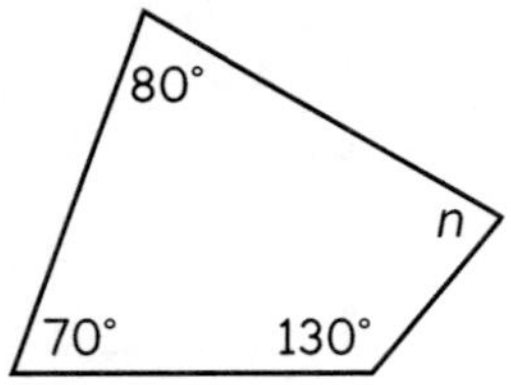

$n =$ ________

9.

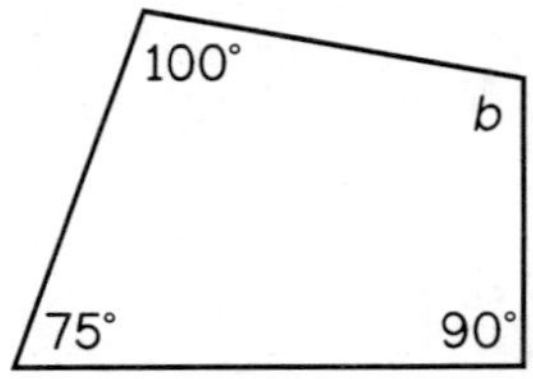

$b =$ ________

10.

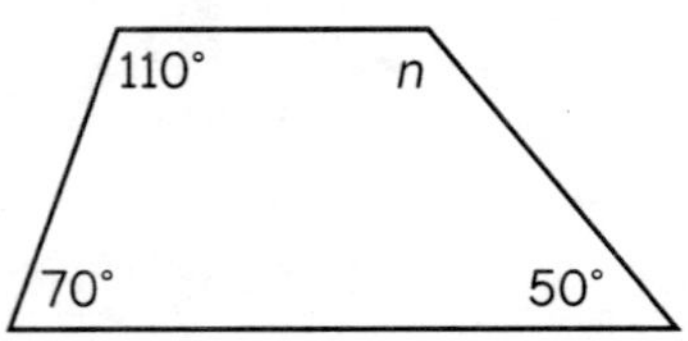

$n =$ ________

11.

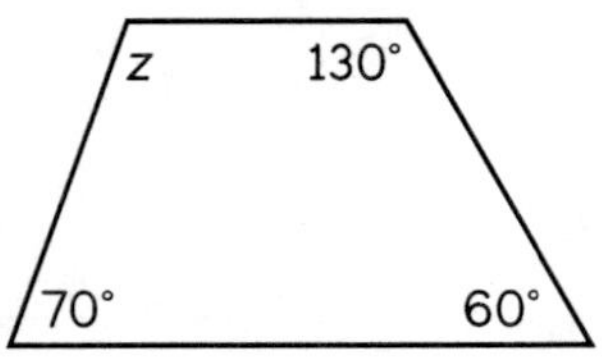

$z =$ ________

12.

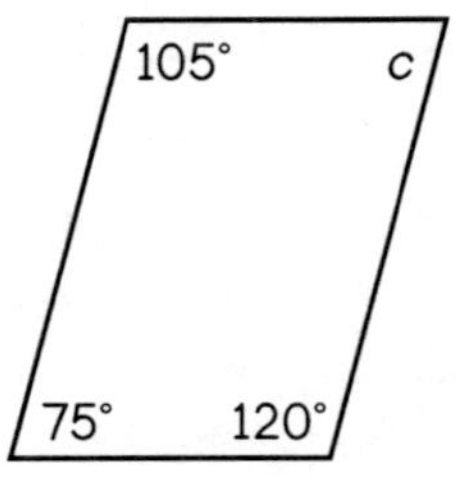

$c =$ ________

Position Words

What to Know

Prepositions are little words whose job it is to tell about the position of someone or something.

Example: *across* the road, *before* the party, *up* in space, *under* my bed

about	around	between	from	on	to
above	at	by	in	over	under
across	before	down	into	past	until
after	behind	during	near	since	up
against	below	except	of	through	with
along	beside	for	off	till	without

Directions: Complete each sentence with a preposition chosen from the box above.

Instrucciones: Completa cada oración con la preposición que elijas de el banco de palabras.

1. Wipe the glasses ______________________ a soft cloth.
2. Wait ______________________ the door, please.
3. The dog went ______________________ the gate.
4. Children are playing ______________________ the beach.
5. We learn to spell ______________________ school.
6. Did you look ______________________ the shed?
7. Ants are crawling ______________________ the hill.
8. A snake slithered ______________________ the log.

Directions: Rewrite the sentences, changing only the prepostion.

Instrucciones: Vuelve a escribir las oraciones, cambiando, solamente, la preposición.

9. A cat sat by the chair. ______________________
10. He ran past the door. ______________________
11. She hid under the tree. ______________________
12. The truck went up the hill. ______________________

Perimeter Math

Directions: Compute the perimeter of each parallelogram. Remember, the perimeter is computed by adding the lengths of each side.

Instrucciones: Calcular el perímetro de cada paralelogramo. Recuerda, el perímetro se calcula sumando las longitudes de cada lado.

1.

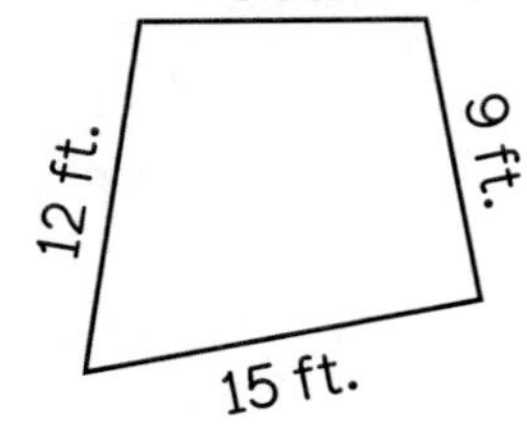

Perimeter = ____________________

2.

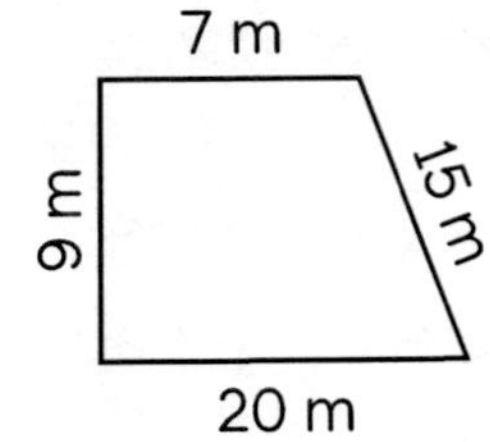

Perimeter = ____________________

3.

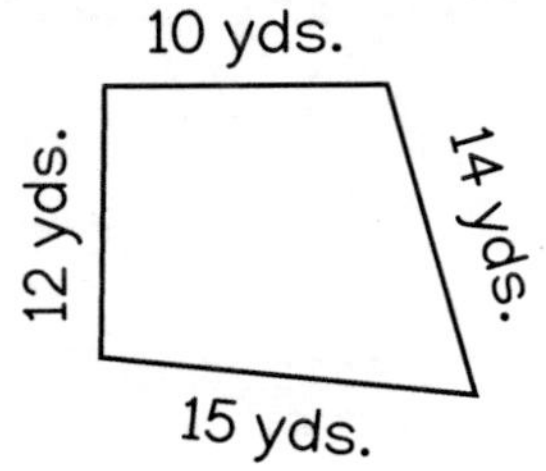

Perimeter = ____________________

4.

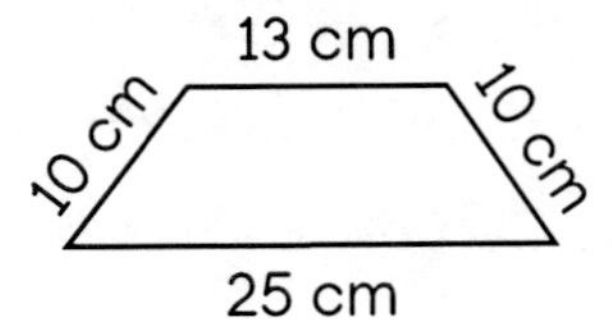

Perimeter = ____________________

5.

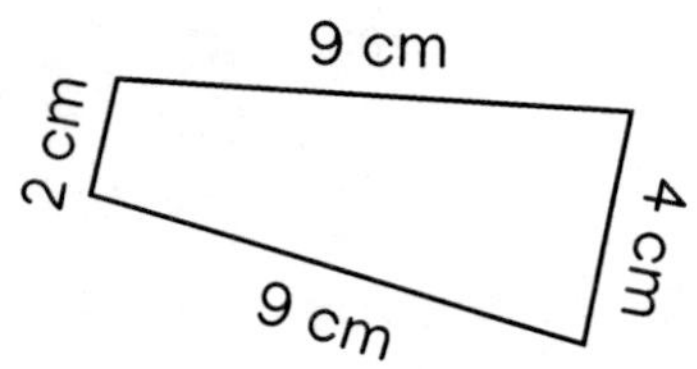

Perimeter = ____________________

6.

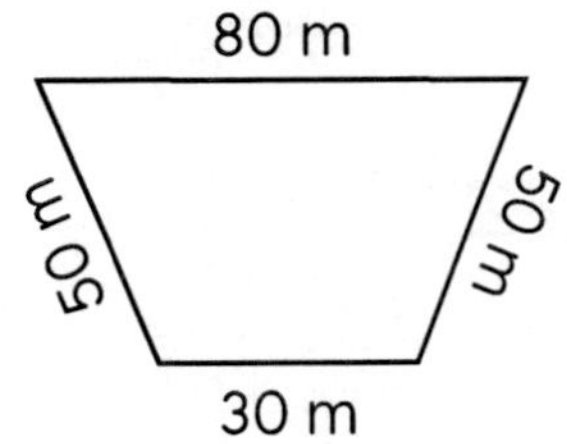

Perimeter = ____________________

7.

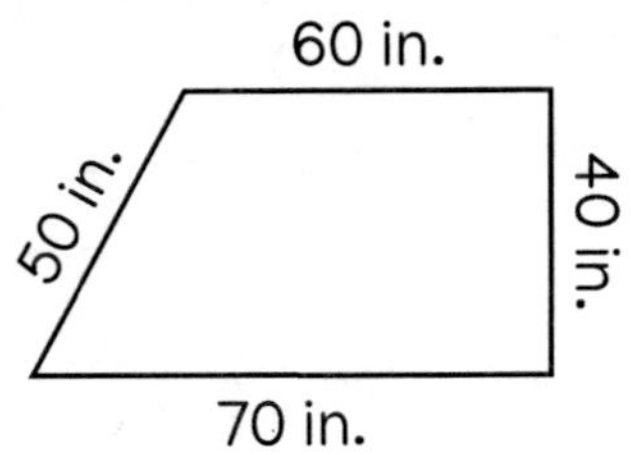

Perimeter = ____________________

8.

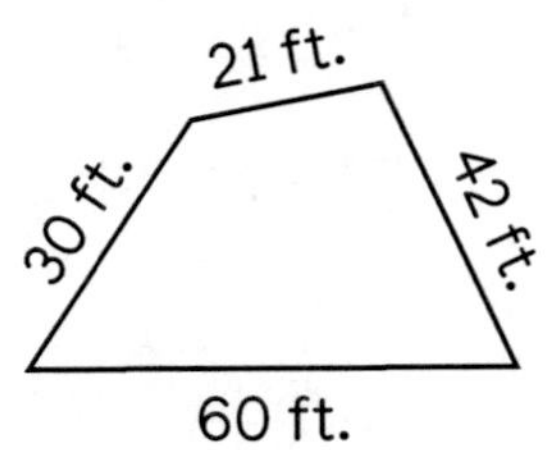

Perimeter = ____________________

Separate Them

What to Know

Commas are used to show short pauses in writing. They are used in various ways, including separating nouns, separating adjectives, and after introductory clauses and phrases.

Directions: Complete each sentence by using three words from the Word Bank. Don't forget to use commas and capitalize the first word of each sentence.

Instrucciones: Completa cada oración usando tres palabras del "Word Bank". No olvides usar comas y mayúsculas en la primera palabra de cada oración.

Word Bank

ash	hammers	pliers	scissors	tulips
corn	oak	rice	skunks	wheat
daffodils	penguins	roses	sycamore	zebras

1. ______________________ are grains.
2. ______________________ are flowers.
3. ______________________ are black and white.
4. ______________________ are tools.
5. ______________________ are trees.

Directions: Each sentence contains a phrase that needs to be set off with commas. Insert the commas before and after the phrase. The first one has been done for you.

Instrucciones: Cada oración contiene una frase que debe separarse con comas. Inserta las comas antes y después de la frase. El ejemplo es para ti.

6. Adelaide, the capital of South Australia, is a beautiful city.
7. Anders Celsius a Swedish astronomer introduced the Celsius scale in 1742.
8. The South Pole a featureless spot in a freezing wilderness was first reached by Amundsen.
9. The toothbrush according to a 17th-century encyclopedia was first invented in China in 1498.
10. Ian one of this class's finest writers has won first prize in the poetry contest.

Race Results

Directions: Mr. Jenson's P.E. class was running a mile-long race. Each student in his class had three weeks to prepare. Some of the students had practiced and some had not. Using the clues below, determine each child's place at the end of the race. Mark the correct boxes with a ✓ and the incorrect boxes with an X.

Instrucciones: La clase de educación física de Sr. Jenson estaba corriendo una carrera de una milla de distancia. Cada alumno de su clase tenía tres semanas para prepararse. Algunos de los estudiantes habían practicado y otros no. Usando las siguientes claves, determina el lugar de cada niño al final de la carrera. Marca las casillas correctas con ✓ y las casillas incorrectas con una X.

1. Paul, who did not beat Emma, placed higher than Dan and Ellis.
2. Ben placed higher than Ellis and Liza.
3. Dan was not in second or last place.
4. Liza saw all of her classmates finish before she did.
5. Emma received the winning ribbon.
6. Ben was not in second or third place.

	1st	2nd	3rd	4th	5th	6th
Ellis						
Liza						
Ben						
Dan						
Paul						
Emma						

"Where" Words

Directions: We can use special words to show direction and position. Here are 15 words that do the job of telling you where something is in relation to something else. Find and circle each word in the puzzle.

Instrucciones: Podemos usar palabras especiales para mostrar dirección y posición. Aquí hay 15 palabras que sirven para decirte dónde está algo en relación con otra cosa. Encuentra y haz un círculo en cada una de las palabras en el rompecabezas.

ABOVE	AROUND	BESIDE	NEAR	OVER
ACROSS	BEHIND	INSIDE	OFF	THROUGH
AFTER	BELOW	INTO	OUTSIDE	UNDER

A	B	O	V	E	P	I	N	T	O
R	E	V	D	N	I	H	E	B	U
O	L	E	R	N	G	E	A	P	T
U	O	R	S	U	O	S	R	I	S
N	W	I	O	F	F	T	I	O	I
D	D	R	A	C	R	O	S	S	D
E	H	N	S	B	E	S	I	D	E
T	U	N	D	E	R	E	T	F	A

What's Left?

What is this type of word called? Find the letters that are **not circled** in the puzzle above. Put them in order to spell the name for this type of word.

It's Your Turn

Imagine you are giving someone directions to find a favorite thing in your house. Write a sentence describing where that thing is. Use at least three direction or position words in your sentence.

Standard and Expanded

Directions: Write each number in standard form, then solve problem 5.

Instrucciones: Escribe cada oración de manera estándar, luego resuelve el problema 5.

1. one thousand, four hundred three

2. two hundred thirty-seven thousand, nine hundred seventy

3. 2 thousands, 2 hundreds, 2 ones

4. 80 thousands, 9 hundreds, 1 ten, 8 ones

5. Kasey bought a present for her mother. She gave the cashier 4 tens and 7 ones. How much did it cost if she had the exact amount?

Directions: Write each number in expanded form, then solve problem 10.

Instrucciones: Escribe cada número de manera expandida, luego resuelve el problema 10.

6. 1,256,753

7. 38,281

8. twenty-two thousand, six hundred

9. eight hundred forty thousand, three

10. Grant wants to buy a CD for $16.99. If he saves $4.00 a week, how many weeks will it take him to save enough money to buy the CD?

Story Types

What to Know

Fiction is a story from someone's imagination.
Nonfiction is a story that is true.

Directions: Read each sentence and decide if it would be found in a fiction or nonfiction book. Write your answer on the line. The first one has been done for you.

Instrucciones: Lea cada oración y decide si se encontraría en un libro de ficción o de no ficción. Escribe "fiction" o "nonfiction" en la línea. El ejemplo es para ti.

1. Columbus is the capital city of Ohio. nonfiction
2. The Nile River is the longest river in Africa. ______________
3. It was a very stormy night when the aliens landed. ______________
4. Space Rangers from planet Zoar came to the rescue. ______________
5. Your heart beats about 76 times a minute. ______________
6. Noisy squirrels threw a party in the forest glade. ______________

Directions: Read each paragraph below and decide if it is *instructional* (describes a process) or *informative* (reports the details of a significant event). Circle the correct answer.

Instrucciones: Lee cada párrafo y decide si es *Instructional* (describe un proceso) o *Informative* (reporta los detalles de un hecho significativo). Haz un círculo alrededor de la respuesta correcta.

To make a grilled cheese sandwich, you need two slices of bread, cheese, butter, a knife, a stove, and a frying pan. First, butter one side of each piece of bread. Next, place one piece, buttered side down, in the frying pan. Then, put one or two slices of cheese on that piece of bread. After that, place the other piece of bread on top, buttered side up. Grill each side for two or three minutes. Now you are ready to eat!

7. **Instructional** or **Informative**

Florence Griffith-Joyner was once the fastest woman in the world. During the 1988 Summer Olympic Games, her speed, strength, and style helped her win three gold medals. Nicknamed "Flo-Jo," she was known for her beautiful, long hair and brightly colored fingernails. After she retired from competition, "Flo-Jo" wrote children's books, designed uniforms for athletes, and served on the President's Council on Physical Fitness and Sports.

8. **Instructional** or **Informative**

Angles and Primes

Directions: Estimate the degrees of each angle, then solve problem 5.

Instrucciones: Estima los grados de cada ángulo, luego resuelve el problema 5.

1.

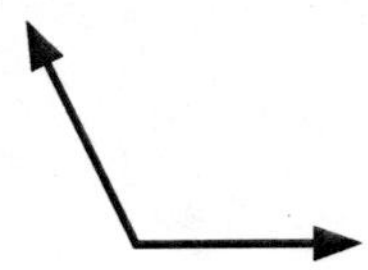

60° 80° 120°

2.

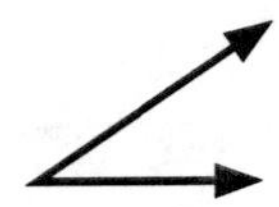

10° 40° 90°

3.

92° 120° 168°

4.

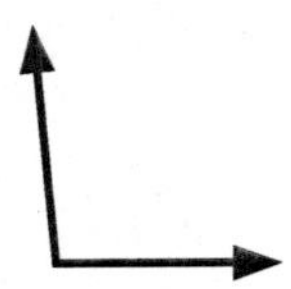

85°

90°

95°

5. Julio bought a 12-pack of soda for $5.40. How much did each soda cost?

____

Directions: Circle the prime number in each group. Then solve problem 10.

Instrucciones: Haz un círculo alrededor del número primo de cada grupo. Luego resuelve el problema 10.

6. 23 46 21

7. 27 19 51

8. 11 39 105

9. 21 57 37

10. A car travels 65 mph. How far will it go in 8 hours?

____

Figurative Feet

What to Know

The words *literal* and *figurative* are opposites. A literal description describes an event exactly as it happens. A figurative description uses a figure of speech to give you an impression about what is happening.

Example: Joe jumped in with both feet.

(literal) Joe jumped into a pool and his feet landed in the water.

(figurative) Joe is trying something new. Instead of starting cautiously, he is getting involved quickly and completely.

Directions: Read the paragraph. Find and underline four examples of figurative descriptions. (There are more than four to find.) For each one, explain what is really being said.

Instrucciones: Lee el párrafo. Encuentra y subraya los cuatro ejemplos de descripciones figurativas. (Hay más de cuatro para encontrar). Por cada una, explica lo que realmente se está diciendo.

Felicia Foote felt like she had the world at her feet. Things could not be going any better for her. Felicia had just gotten a big loan to start her new business. For too long, Felicia had relied on her family to help her. She knew it was now time to stand on her own two feet and make her own way. Felicia threw caution to the wind and gave her all to this new business opportunity. She felt that she was good at thinking on her feet and she would succeed eventually. Whatever difficulties she might have, she was confident she would be able to land on her feet.

Example	What It Really Means
1.	
2.	
3.	
4.	

Many Variables

Directions: Find the value of each expression. Then, solve problem 5.

Instrucciones: Encuentra el valor de cada expresión. Luego, soluciona el problema 5.

1. $x - 12 = 88$

$x =$ __________

2. $7 \times z = 49$

$z =$ __________

3. $144 \div y = 12$

$y =$ __________

4. $n + 120 + 40 = 241$

$n =$ __________

5. On the way to Mrs. Ward's classroom, the new student will pass four other rooms. Mrs. Proctor's room is next to Mrs. Baker's room. Mrs. Morgan's room is between Mrs. Proctor's and Mrs. Prince's room. Mrs. Prince's room is not next to Mrs. Ward's room. Which classroom is beside Mrs. Ward's room?

				Mrs. Ward

____

Directions: Solve for *n*. Then, solve problem 10.

Instrucciones: Resuelve para *n*. Luego, resuelve el problema 10.

6. $48 - 12 = 6 \times n$

$n =$ __________

7. $26 \times 3 = 122 - n$

$n =$ __________

8. $23 + 15 = 40 - n$

$n =$ __________

9. $72 \div 9 = 100 - n$

$n =$ __________

10. Sir Francis Drake explored California in 1579, and 28 years later, Jamestown was settled by Captain John Smith. What year was that?

____

Air Tour

Directions: Read the following story. Use the Mini Dictionary to help you.

Instrucciones: Lee el siguiente cuento a continuación. Usa el "Mini Dictionary" para ayudarte.

Mini Dictionary

delta – a triangle of land built at the mouth of a river by the flowing water
hydroelectric – electricity generated by the movement of water
hydroplane – an airplane that is equipped to land on water
isthmus – a narrow piece of land connecting two large bodies of land
strait – a narrow passage of water connecting two large bodies of water
tributary – a river or stream flowing into a larger river or lake

A bus took us to the ______________ (1) between the two big islands, where a boat was waiting for us. I'd never taken a boat ride to get into the air, but that's exactly what we did: it took us out to a ______________ (2) just sitting there floating! After we climbed into the air, I saw two of the smaller islands connected by a land bridge, which the pilot told us is called an ______________ (3). Before long, we were flying over the mainland. We started at the south, where I could see the ______________ (4) of a big river. We followed the river north. At one point, I saw a big ______________ (5) dam, which the pilot said provided power for a whole city! As we continued north, I saw one ______________ (6) flowing into the river, then another, then a third. I was sorry when the plane circled back to where we'd started for a landing. It was a great flight!

Directions: Match each idea to the correct word. Place the letter of the answer on the line.

Instrucciones: Relaciona cada idea con la palabra correcta. Coloque la letra de la repuesta en el línea.

________	7. thin section of land	**a.** tributary
________	8. travels in the air, lands in the water	**b.** hydroelectric
________	9. makes power from water	**c.** hydroplane
________	10. thin section of water	**d.** strait
________	11. water on three sides	**e.** isthmus
________	12. flows into a river	**f.** delta

Shade and Show

Directions: Shade each circle to show the fraction. Then, write > or < to make each comparison correct. The first one has been done for you.

Instrucciones: Sombrea cada círculo para mostrar la fracción. Luego, escribe > o < para hacer cada comparación correcta. El ejemplo es para ti.

1.

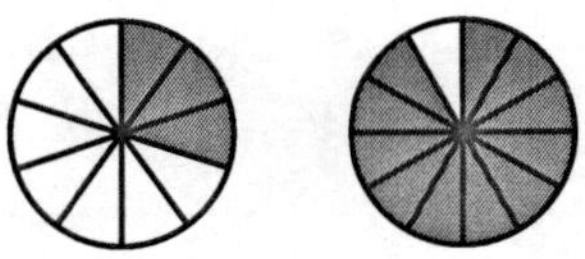

$\frac{3}{10}$ (<) $\frac{11}{12}$

2.

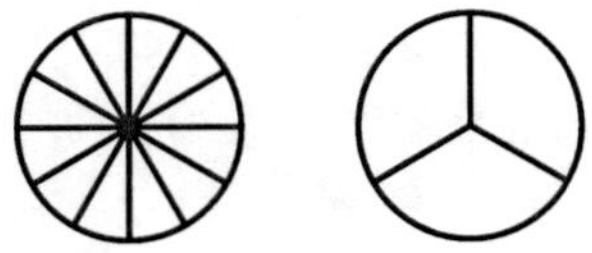

$\frac{6}{12}$ ◯ $\frac{2}{3}$

3.

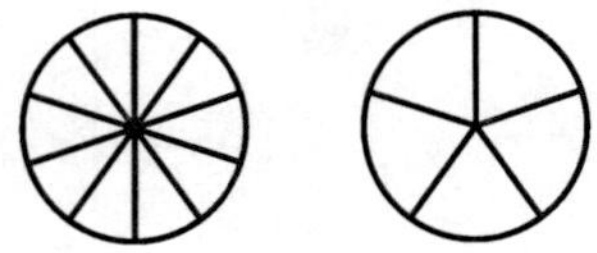

$\frac{8}{10}$ ◯ $\frac{2}{5}$

4.

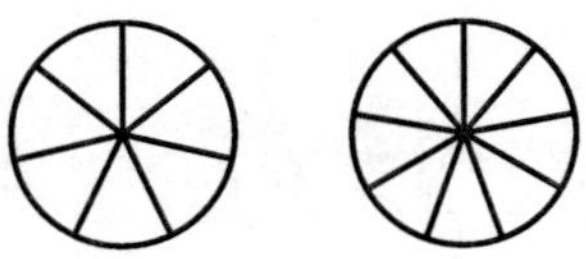

$\frac{2}{7}$ ◯ $\frac{4}{9}$

5.

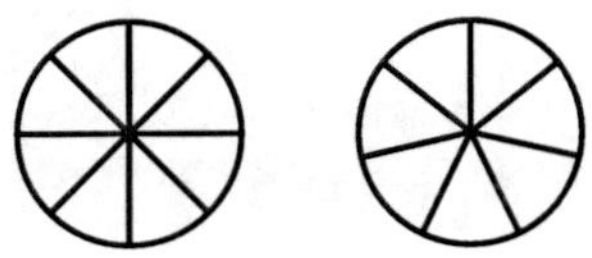

$\frac{1}{8}$ ◯ $\frac{3}{7}$

6.

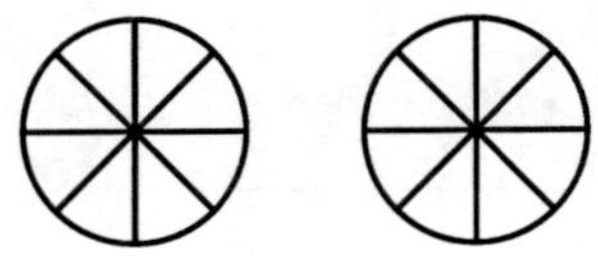

$\frac{3}{8}$ ◯ $\frac{7}{8}$

7.

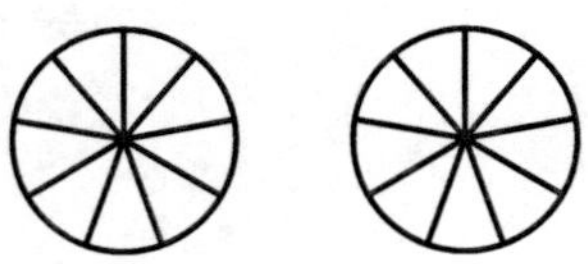

$\frac{8}{9}$ ◯ $\frac{7}{9}$

8.

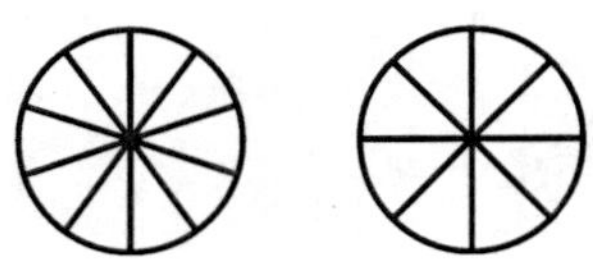

$\frac{6}{10}$ ◯ $\frac{4}{8}$

9.

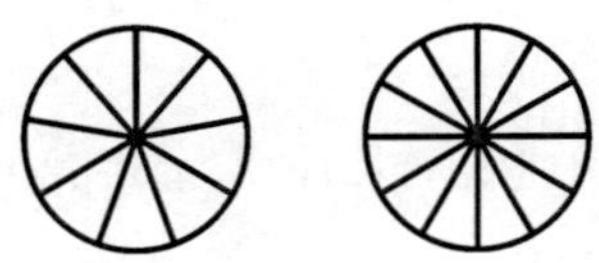

$\frac{6}{9}$ ◯ $\frac{10}{12}$

10.

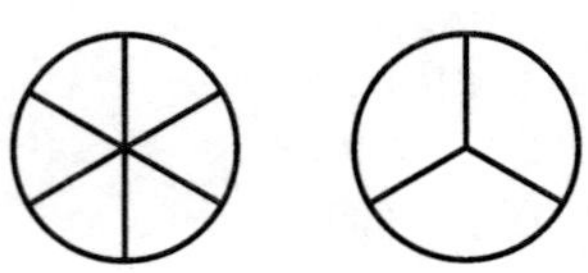

$\frac{1}{6}$ ◯ $\frac{1}{3}$

11.

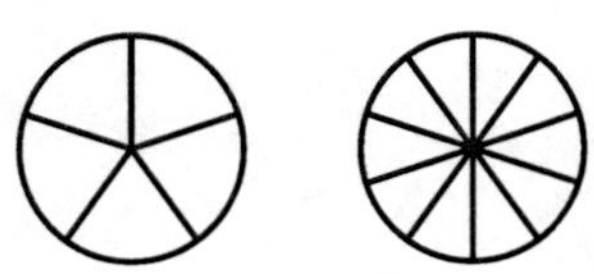

$\frac{4}{5}$ ◯ $\frac{2}{10}$

12.

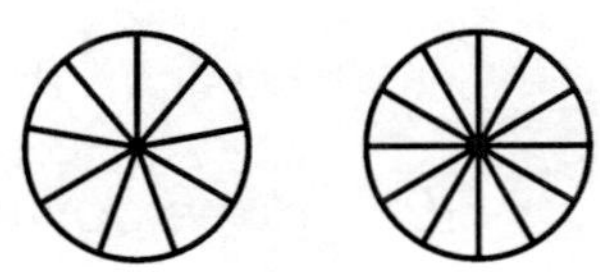

$\frac{3}{9}$ ◯ $\frac{3}{12}$

Noun Types

Directions: Write each noun under the correct heading. Add two more nouns under each heading.

Instrucciones: Escribe cada sustantivo bajo el título correcto. Agrega dos sustantivos más, debajo de cada título.

book	cat	cousin	desk	girl	happiness
Houston	love	Spain	country	student	wisdom

Person	Place	Thing	Idea
Add two more.	Add two more.	Add two more.	Add two more.

Directions: Write a sentence with each verb.

Instrucciones: Escribe una oración con cada uno de los verbos.

1. has taken ____________________
2. bought ____________________
3. has flown ____________________
4. went ____________________
5. have seen ____________________
6. walked ____________________
7. was going ____________________
8. is ____________________

Take the Plunge

Directions: Look at these groups of letters to solve the puzzles. They are in order and no letters have been omitted, but most cannot be read left to right. Patterns may be horizontal or vertical. Pay close attention to the clues provided. The first one has been done for you.

Instrucciones: Mira estos grupos de letras para resolver los rompecabezas. Están en orden y no se han omitido ninguna letra, pero la mayoría no se puede leer de izquierda a derecha. Los patrones pueden ser horizontales o verticales. Presta mucha atención a las claves proporcionadas. El ejemplo es para ti.

1.

S	D	I
W	+	V
I	G	I
M	N	N
M	I	G

water sports

swimming and diving

2.

R	I	V	E	R
S	L	A	K	E
S	S	E	A	S

bodies of water

3.

T	E	S	T
U	K	T	H
C	I	R	G
K	P	A	I

diving body positions

4.

B	A	T	H	I	N
G	S	U	I	T	G
O	G	G	L	E	S

swimmer's uniform

5.

S	A	A
P	N	M
E	D	I
E	S	N
D	T	A

needed to win

6.

N	V	R	W	M	L	N
E	E	S	I	A	O	E

important safety rule

Idiom Crossword

What to Know

An **idiom** is an expression with special meaning that cannot be understood by looking at the individual words.

Example: "With flying colors" means with ease and success.

Directions: Fill in the blanks with the words in the Word Bank to complete the idioms. Then, use the missing words to complete the crossword puzzle.

Instrucciones: Llena los espacios en blanco con las palabras del "Word Bank" para completar los modismos. Luego, usa las palabras que faltan para completar el crucigrama.

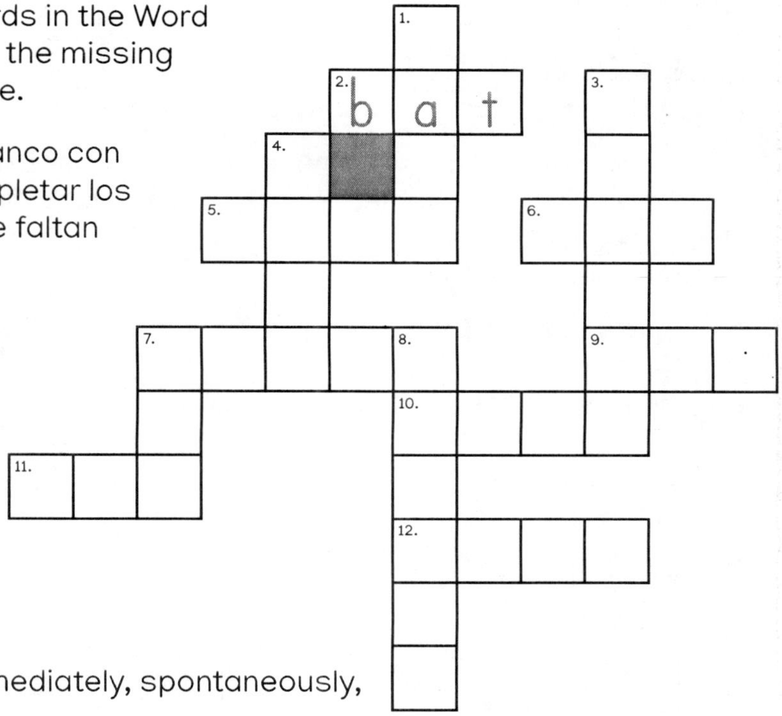

Word Bank

bait	gun	hour	switch
~~bat~~	hat	leg	time
bit	horns	lost	wire
double			

Across

2. Right off the ___bat___ – immediately, spontaneously, and without delay
5. Make up for __________ time – to do much of something or to do something fast
6. Jump the __________ – to be hasty and do or say something before it is time
7. Take the bull by the __________ – to take action and stop hesitating
9. Shake a __________ – to hurry up and go faster
10. Down to the __________ – running out of time or at the last minute
11. Chomp at the __________ – to be impatient to start and enthusiastic to do something
12. Procrastination is the thief of __________ – If you wait, you may not have enough time left to do it once you finally get started.

Down

1. Fish or cut __________ – Do one thing or another, but stop delaying.
3. On the __________ – very quickly and at a fast pace
4. In the eleventh __________ – at the last possible moment
7. At the drop of a __________ – right away, immediately
8. Asleep at the __________ – not attending to a job or not reacting quickly

Sales Figures

Directions: The owners of a car lot lost all of their receipts for the past six months. Help them work with what they have to figure out how many cars they sold and how much they need to pay their salespeople.

Instrucciones: Los dueños de un lote de autos perdieron todos sus recibos de los últimos seis meses. Ayúdales a trabajar con lo que tienen para averiguar cuántos autos vendieron y cuánto necesitan pagar a sus vendedores.

Part 1: How Many Cars>

March was a good month because they sold twice as many cars as they did in July. They sold the same number of cars in April as in June. In April there were 20 cars fewer sold than in August. In May they sold 70 cars. That was exactly 25 more cars than were sold in both July and August.

1. Cars sold in March: ____________________
2. Cars sold in April: ____________________
3. Cars sold in May: ____________________
4. Cars sold in June: ____________________
5. Cars sold in July: ____________________
6. Cars sold in August: ____________________
7. Total cars sold from March to August: ____________

Part 2: How Much Money?

The top three salespeople at the car lot are Rick, Kelly, and Dahlia. From March to August, Rick's sales were $60,000 higher than Kelly's. However, Dahlia's sales were twice as much as Rick's. In fact, she broke the company sales record by selling $220,000 worth of cars from March to August.

8. Sales for Dahlia: ____________________
9. Sales for Rick: ____________________
10. Sales for Kelly: ____________________

Making Inferences

Directions: Study the picture below. Make inferences about what is happening in the picture. Provide evidence to support each idea. An example is given.

Instrucciones: Estudia la imagen de abajo. Hace inferencias sobre lo que está sucediendo en la imagen. Proporciona evidencia para apoyar cada idea. Se da un ejemplo.

Example Inference: These two people are friends.

Evidence: They are smiling and interacting.

Your Inference #1

____

____

Evidence

____

____

Your Inference #2

____

____

Evidence

____

____

Recipe Math

Directions: Mark is the manager of The Eatery. He often has to change recipes to suit the number of people he estimates he will have to serve. Complete the tables in order to change the recipes to serve different numbers of people. Some answers are given.

Instrucciones: Mark es el gerente de The Eatery. A menudo tiene que cambiar recetas para adaptarse a la cantidad de personas que estima que tendrá que atender. Completa las tablas para cambiar las recetas para servir a diferentes cantidades de personas. Se dan algunas respuestas.

Party Fruit Salad

Serves 8 people	Serves 24 people
6 cups watermelon	
2 cups raisins	
3 apples	
$\frac{1}{2}$ cup cherries	
1 lb. strawberries	3 lbs. strawberries
1 mango	

Rule: ______________________

Turkey Loaf

Serves 8 people	Serves 64 people
2 lbs. ground turkey	
$\frac{1}{4}$ cup mashed potatoes	2 cups mashed potatoes
5 tbsp. breadcrumbs	
$\frac{1}{3}$ cup onions	
1 egg	
1 dash salt	
1 dash pepper	

Rule: ______________________

Chili

Serves 8 people	Serves ______ people
2 lbs. ground turkey	1 lb. ground turkey
8 oz. cooked black beans	
16 oz. cooked kidney beans	
$\frac{1}{3}$ tsp. fresh garlic	
$\frac{1}{2}$ tsp. salt	$\frac{1}{4}$ tsp. salt
$\frac{1}{5}$ lb. snap beans	
1 package chili powder	
1 cup salsa	

Rule: ______________________

Past Poetry

Directions: This famous poem by Robert Frost captures the feelings that go into the choices we make in our lives. Think about some of the decisions you have made in your life so far, then write your response below.

Instrucciones: Este famoso poema de Robert Frost captura los sentimientos que acompañan a las elecciones que hacemos en nuestra vida. Piensa en algunas de las decisiones que has hecho en tu vida hasta ahora, luego escribe tu respuesta.

The Road Not Taken

Two roads diverged in a yellow wood,
And sorry I could not travel both
And be one traveler, long I stood
And looked down one as far as I could
To where it bent in the undergrowth;

Then took the other, as just as fair,
And having perhaps the better claim,
Because it was grassy and wanted wear;
Though as for that the passing there
Had worn them really about the same,

And both that morning equally lay
In leaves no step had trodden black.
Oh, I kept the first for another day!
Yet knowing how way leads on to way,
I doubted if I should ever come back.

I shall be telling this with a sigh
Somewhere ages and ages hence:
Two roads diverged in a wood, and I –
I took the road less traveled by,
And that has made all the difference.

Decisions I have made today:

___

___

Decisions I have made in the past year:

___

___

Decisions I have made in my life:

___

___

How do you feel about these decisions?

___

___

Volume Cubes

Directions: Compute the volume of each cube.

Instrucciones: Calcula el volumen de cada cubo.

What to Know The **volume of a cube** is computed by multiplying the length of one side times itself twice. ($V = s \times s \times s$ *or* $V = s^3$ *or* Volume = length of side cubed)

1.

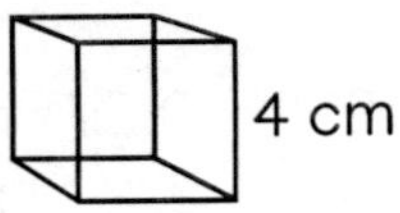

____

2.

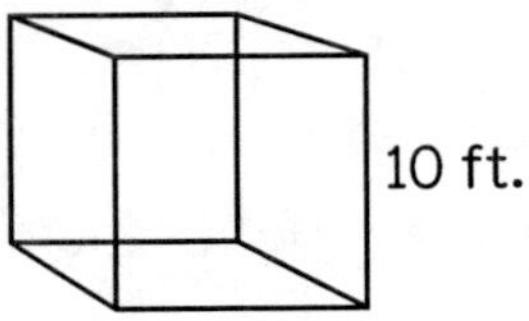

____

3.

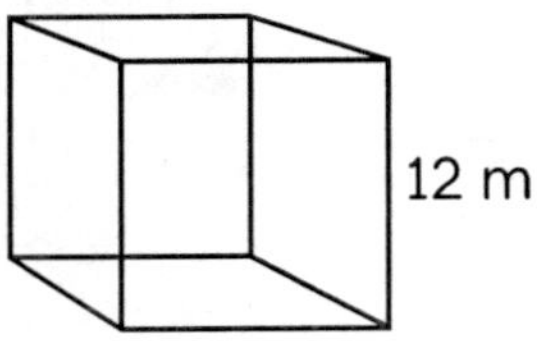

____

4.

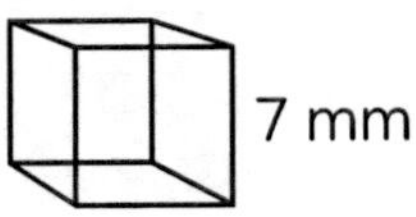

____

5.

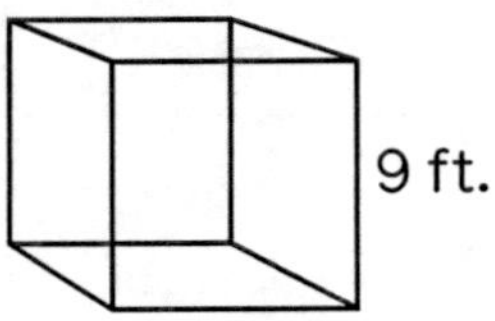

____

6.

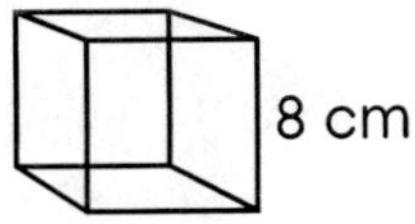

____

7.

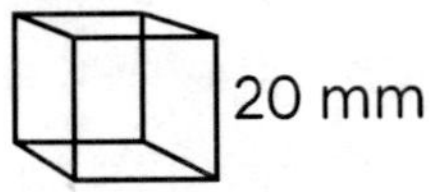

____

8.

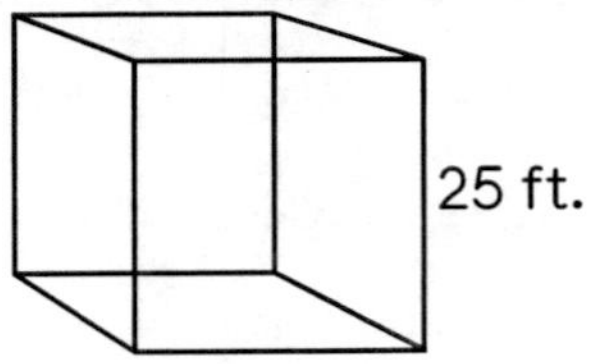

____

9.

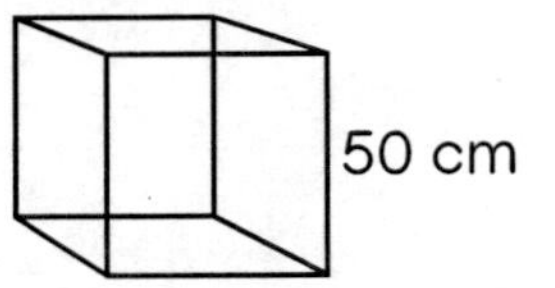

____

10.

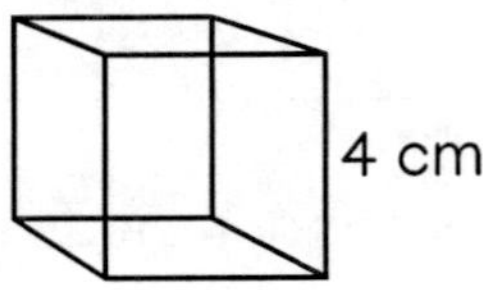

____

TV Review

Directions: Choose a favorite TV show about a family. Then, complete the following review.

Instrucciones: Elije tu programa favorito de televisión acerca de una familia. Luego, completa la siguiente opinión.

Name of program: ______________________________

1. Summary of episode: ______________________________

____

____

2. Explain how the show depicts the mother. ______________________________

____

3. Explain how the show depicts the father. ______________________________

____

4. Name a child who is a main character in this episode. ______________________________

   a. What problem or dilemma do they face in this episode? ______________________________

   ____

   b. How is it resolved? ______________________________

   ____

5. Does the program portray a realistic family? Circle **Yes** or **No**. Explain.

____

____

6. How is your family like this TV family? ______________________________

____

How is it different? ______________________________

____

Going the Distance

Math Facts

- The **circumference** (C) is the distance around a circle. (*Formula:* $C = \pi \times d$, $\pi = 3.14$)
- The **radius** (r) is the distance from the center of a circle to any point on the circle.
- The **diameter** (d) is a line segment extending from one side of the circle to the other through the center of the circle.
- The **diameter** is twice the radius. (*Formula:* $d = 2 \times r$)

Directions: Label the circumference, the radius, and the diameter on these circles.

Instrucciones: Etiqueta la circunferencia, el radio y el diámetro en estos círculos.

1.

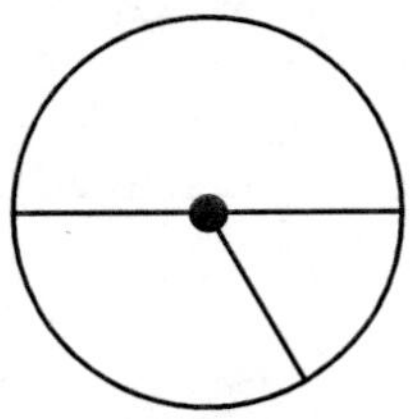

2.

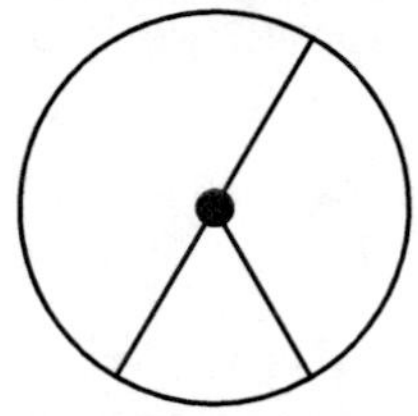

3.

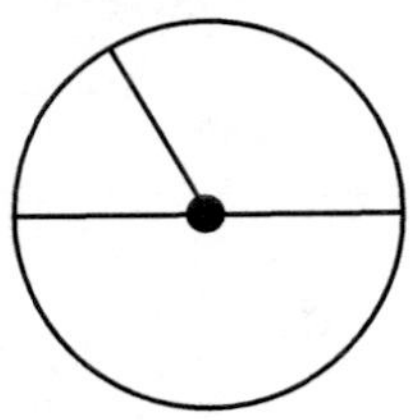

4.

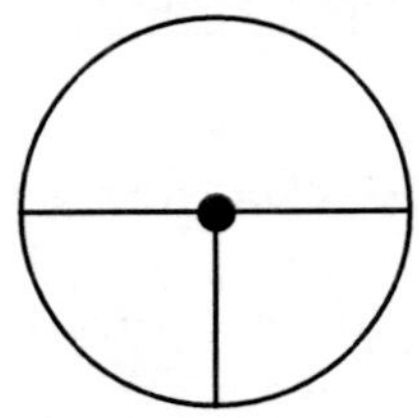

Directions: Use the information on the circles to find the values. Round each circumference to the nearest whole number.

Instrucciones: Usa la información de los círculos para encontrar los valores. Redondea cada circunferencia al número entero más cercano.

5.

r = ______________

d = ______________

C = ______________

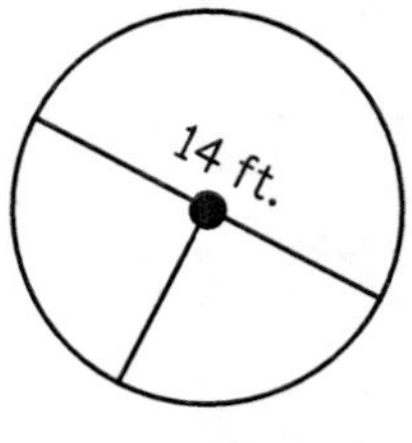

6.

r = ______________

d = ______________

C = ______________

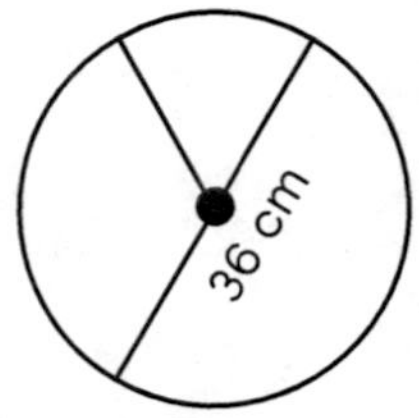

7.

r = ______________

d = ______________

C = ______________

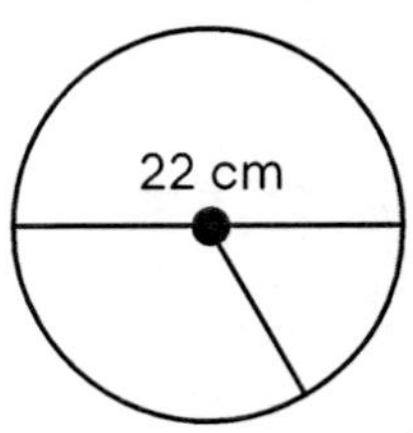

8.

r = ______________

d = ______________

C = ______________

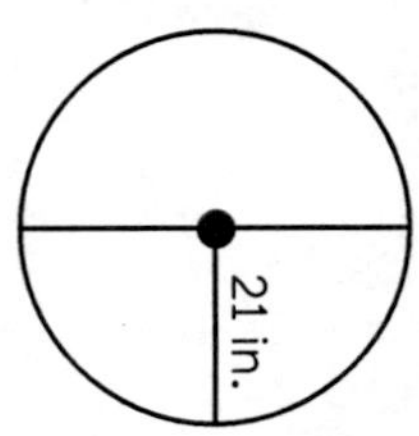

What's the Purpose?

Directions: Read the story and answer the questions below.

Instrucciones: Lee el cuento y responde las preguntas a continuación.

I hope this story does not bore you or make you sleepy. This is something about something kids do. Grownups do it, too. So do dogs, rabbits, and snakes. Babies do it before they are even born. And if you see or hear someone else do it, you will probably not be able to stop yourself from doing it. What could it be? What is this story about?

This story is about yawning. Yawning is something we do about 15 times a day. We do it most often before we go to sleep. We also seem to do it a lot when we are bored. But *why* do we do it?

The answer is that we do not know. There are many ideas about why we yawn, but we don't know for sure. Yawning brings oxygen into our bodies, so one idea is that we do it when we need more oxygen. We also yawn more when we are warm. Another idea is that we yawn to cool our brains. It sounds strange, but it may be true.

The other weird thing about yawning is that people yawn when they see or hear other people yawn. Why does this happen? Once again, no one knows. Yawning is a mystery. Is it an exciting mystery, or is it one that makes you yawn?

1. What is the purpose of each paragraph in this story? For each paragraph number, write a short sentence or phrase to explain what it is about. The first one is done for you.

   Paragraph #1: to make the reader want to find out what the story is about

   Paragraph #2: ____________________

   Paragraph #3: ____________________

   Paragraph #4: ____________________

2. In your own words, what is the main purpose of the whole story?

   ____

   ____

3. Is the mystery of yawning interesting to you, or is it boring? Explain.

   ____

   ____

   ____

An All-Time Great

Directions: Use the code to fill in the blanks and identify the person who is widely regarded as one of the best soccer players of all time.

Instrucciones: Usa el código para llenar los espacios en blanco e identificar a la persona que es ampliamente considerada como uno de los mejores futbolistas de todos los tiempos.

A	C	D	E	I	M	N	O	R	S	T	B	Z	L	P	F	W
1	2	3	4	5	6	7	8	9	10	11	12	13	14	15	16	17

This soccer player was born in ____ ____ ____ ____ ____ ____ (12 9 1 13 5 14). At age fifteen, he played

for the ____ ____ ____ ____ ____ ____ (10 1 7 11 8 10), a professional soccer club. He was a talented

____ ____ ____ ____ ____ ____ ____ (16 8 9 17 1 9 3) and led his team to three ____ ____ ____ ____ ____ (17 8 9 14 3)

championships. He ____ ____ ____ ____ ____ ____ ____ (9 4 11 5 9 4 3) in 1973, but in 1975, he returned

to play for the New York ____ ____ ____ ____ ____ ____ (2 8 10 6 8 10). The full

name of this amazing athlete is ____ ____ ____ ____ ____ (4 3 10 8 7)

____ ____ ____ ____ ____ ____ ____ (1 9 1 7 11 4 10) ____ ____ (3 8)

____ ____ ____ ____ ____ ____ ____ ____ ____ ____ (7 1 10 2 5 6 4 7 11 8), but he is

best known by his nickname, ____ ____ ____ ____ (15 4 14 4).

More Droodles

What to Know

Droodles are artistic interpretations of brainteasers. Pictures or illustrations are used to present information. Symbols may represent different things depending on the context. Word clues may be added.

Directions: What could these droodles be? Write your answers on the lines.

Instrucciones: ¿Qué podrían ser estos garabatos? Escribe tus respuestas en las líneas.

Droodle #1

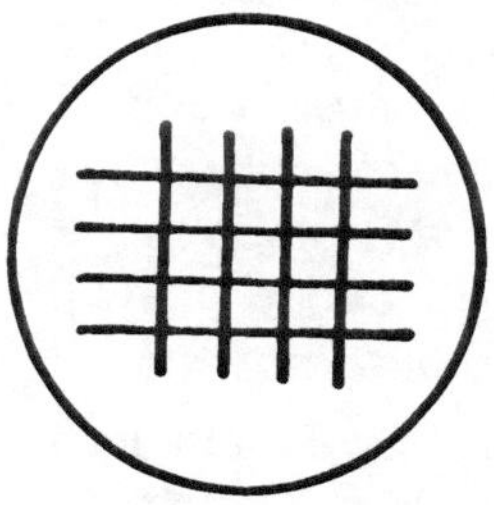

What could it be? ______________________

____

Droodle #2

What could it be? ______________________

____

Droodle #3

What could it be? ______________________

____

Droodle #4

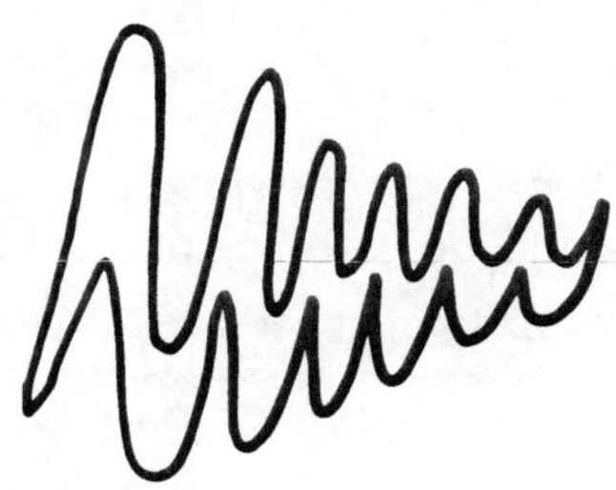

What could it be? ______________________

____

Droodle #5

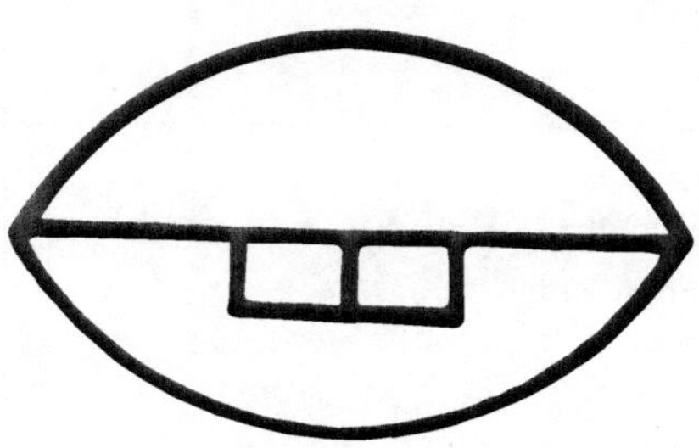

What could it be? ______________________

____

Droodle #6

What could it be? ______________________

____

Summer Reading List

Uno de los mejores modos de promover el desarrollo educativo durante el verano es mediante la lectura. Afortunadamente, existe una gran variedad de fantásticos libros ilustrados y de pasta dura que podrían interesas y cautivar a tu joven lector. Por favor, lee las reseñas y/o lee los libros tú mismo antes de presentárselos a tu hijo, con el fin de determinar si son adecuados para él.

Si lo deseas, puedes utilizar este gráfico (y el que figura en la páginas 93–94) para mantenerte organizado. Utiliza la columna de **Dates** para anotar el día en que tu hijo leyó el libro o cuándo debería devolverlo en la biblioteca. Utiliza la columna de **Notes** como ayuda para recordar lo que has leído en las reseñas de otros lectores o lo que tu hijo pensó del libro tras leerlo.

Dates	Book Information	Notes
	The Crossover by Kwame Alexander Josh Bell's father played in the pros long ago, and his brother is a really good player, too. But what Josh can do on the basketball court is special, and everyone knows it. Life off the court, however, is not always an easy game for Josh to play or even figure out. Poetically told in dynamic and compelling language, this popular novel is a great read even for those who don't love basketball. *Themes:* family relationships, coming of age, change, loss, living in the spotlight	
	The One and Only Ivan by Katherine Applegate Through the eyes, ears, and thoughts of a warm-hearted gorilla named Ivan, we learn what life is like for a group of animals in a long-failing circus. Then one day, Ivan must find in himself the leader he was born to be in order to fulfill a promise to an old friend. *Themes:* home, family/friendship/community, identity, memory, animal rights	
	Jim Thorpe's Bright Path by Joseph Bruchac Jim Thorpe is widely considered the greatest Native American athlete of all time. This book focuses on how his boyhood set the stage for his international fame. *Themes:* importance of hard work, tenacity, competition	
	Leonardo: Beautiful Dreamer by Robert Byrd This is a fascinating biography of Leonardo da Vinci, who was a painter, sculptor, scientist, mathematician, and architect. It features award-winning illustrations. *Themes:* inventor's mind, hard work, tenacity	
	Chasing Redbird by Sharon Creech A powerful mystery story about Zinnia Taylor, a country girl who discovers a hidden trail and, along the way, discovers a lot about herself. *Themes:* family secrets, finding yourself, mystery	
	Bud, Not Buddy by Christopher Paul Curtis In the midst of a nation's Great Depression, Bud (do not call him Buddy) has been in and out of homes ever since his mother passed away. After a terrible stint with a family of bullies, Bud sets out on his own to find the father he's never known. All he has are his street smarts and a band flier his mother kept. Is the man on the flier Bud's father? What happens next is an adventure as funny, sweet, sensitive, and nuanced as the book's main character. *Themes:* family, coming of age, poverty, race, finding one's place	

Summer Reading List *(cont.)*

Dates	Book Information	Notes
	Rodzina by Karen Cushman Set in the 1880s, this is the story of a twelve-year-old girl who joins an orphan train and travels across the United States in search of a family. Along the way, she meets many people and has many experiences. All the while, she holds on to the past and family she once knew and wonders what family she will have in the future. *Themes:* abandonment, values, dreams	
	Matilda by Roald Dahl Matilda Wormwood loves to read, but her TV-watching parents don't approve. Only Miss Honey, Matilda's teacher, recognizes her true genius. Matilda uses her head to help defeat the evildoers who are after Miss Honey. *Themes:* problem solving, caring, the power of positivity	
	Out of My Mind by Sharon M. Draper Melody is extremely intelligent and thoughtful, but no one knows it because her cerebral palsy severely limits her ability to communicate. Then one day she receives a special device that allows her to get her thoughts out of her mind and show who she truly is and has always been. *Themes:* ability/disability, communication, family/friendship, acceptance/rejection	
	The City of Ember by Jeanne DuPrau The city of Ember was built long ago, and no one who lives there has known any other place. This city is lit solely by electricity, and the ancient generator that powers everything has been falling apart for a while. Once it fails, the city will be plunged into a darkness that cannot be escaped. Two children work together to solve the mystery of where they are and how they can save a city full of people who are only willing to look as far as the few feet lit in front of them. *Themes:* environmentalism, survival, curiosity, action vs. passivity	
	Escape from Mr. Lemoncello's Library by Chris Grabenstein A contest leads to the opportunity of a lifetime: a chance to be the first to explore (and escape from) a new library designed by the world's greatest game-maker. But can everyone put aside their differences and work together to decipher the clues in time to make their escape? *Themes:* teamwork, friendship, identity, creativity	
	Roller Girl by Victoria Jamieson Astrid and Nicole are best friends, and nothing can change that. Until it does. A trip to see a woman's roller derby sparks an inspiration in Astrid at a time in her life when that is needed. This graphic novel presents a realistic look at how friendships can grow, change, and sometimes disappear when interests begin to diverge. *Themes:* friendship, change, identity, challenging yourself, perseverance, teamwork	
	The Year of Miss Agnes by Kirkpatrick Hill Miss Agnes arrives in a Native American village in 1948 Alaska and has a profound influence on her pupils. *Themes:* learning, trust, friendship	
	The View from Saturday by E.L. Konigsburg Mrs. Olinski's Academic Bowl team beats the older kids and makes history. Each team member has his or her own fascinating story, and together they are unstoppable. *Themes:* learning, trust, friendship	

Summer Reading List *(cont.)*

Dates	Book Information	Notes
	Inside Out and Back Again by Thanhhà Lai A new year brings incredible change for Hà's family, as they must flee Saigon and journey to America. Once there, Hà is an outsider and must face off against bullies, a new language, and her own hard-headedness. This story is told in free-verse poetry that adds depth and beauty to all of Hà's experiences. *Themes:* family, identity, cultural differences, acceptance/rejection, bullying	
	Esperanza Rising by Pam Muñoz Ryan Esperanza's privileged life in Mexico is like a fairy tale. Then tragedy strikes, and she and her mother are forced to flee their comfortable life. In the U.S., they must start from the bottom, working the land for others and facing one hardship after another. In a year of unimaginable pain and growth, Esperanza learns to look beyond herself and to possess a strength she never knew she could. *Themes:* loss, change, identity, poverty, class, strength and courage, coming of age	
	Wonder by R.J. Palacio Auggie was born with craniofacial differences. He feels "normal" at his core, but his appearance makes people uncomfortable and forces them to confront something within themselves. In this beloved and inspiring novel written from multiple points of view, we get to truly "see" Auggie *and* we get to see others seeing him too. *Themes:* support systems, identity, acceptance/rejection, empathy, bullying	
	Holes by Louis Sachar As the result of bad luck, Stanley Yelnats IV finds himself in a miserable juvenile detention center in the middle of the desert. The past and the present are very much intertwined in this impressive tale of a boy who is forced to dig holes and the truth he is able to unearth about himself and everyone else. *Themes:* family/friendship, identity, acceptance/rejection, empathy, bullying	

Aprovechando al máximo la lectura de verano

Cuando lea estos libros con su hijo, es posible que desee hacer las siguientes preguntas. Seguimiento respecto a las respuestas cortas para animar a su hijo a explicar sus pensamientos con mayor detalle.

- ¿Sobre qué es el cuento?
- ¿Dónde sucede el cuento? ¿Cómo es este escenario un "personaje" en el cuento?
- ¿Cuándo tiene lugar el cuento? ¿Por qué es importante el período de tiempo para la trama?
- ¿Quién es un personaje principal en el cuento? ¿Cómo los eventos de la historia hacen que este personaje crezca o cambie a medida que avanza el cuento?
- Nombra un personaje secundario o sustentador. Cómo ellos hacen que ocurran eventos en el cuento, y ¿cómo ayuda o perjudica esto al personaje principal?
- Nombra un conflicto en el cuento. ¿Cómo se resuelve?
- ¿Alguno de los eventos o temas de este cuento te hizo pensar en tu propia vida o examinar tu propia forma de pensar? Explicar.

Read and Do

A continuación, se incluyen algunas ideas divertidas para que tu hijo incremente su lectura. La mayoría implicarán la participación de ambos, pero se encuentran dirigidas hacia él con el fin de incentivar su amor por los libros.

How I Felt ___/___/___	How did this novel make you feel as you read it? Create a page of words, pictures, and colors that you feel describe the mood of the novel.
If It Were Me ___/___/	Imagine that you are stuck in the world of the novel. Which event from the novel would be the most challenging (or enjoyable, frustrating, etc.) for you to deal with? Why?
"Like" I Said ___/___/	Use similes to describe characters, settings, or events from the novel. You might even create a few similes to describe your experience of reading the novel. In all, form five similes and explain each.
Write to the Author ___/___/___	Many authors love to hear from their readers, especially when they hear what people liked best about their books. You can write to an author and send your letter in care of the book's publisher. The publisher's address is listed directly after the title page. Or you may go to the author's website and follow the directions for how to send the author a letter. (To make sure your author is still living, type the author's name into an online search engine.)
A Comic Book ___/___/___	Turn your favorite book into a comic book. Fold at least two sheets of paper in half, and staple them so they make a book. With a ruler and pencil, draw boxes across each page to look like blank comic strips. Then, draw the story of your book as if it were a comic. Draw pictures of your characters, and have words coming out of their mouths—just as in a real comic strip.
Novel Foods ___/___/___	What foods do the characters in your book eat? What do they drink? What are their favorite foods? Decide what foods your characters love. With your parents' help, locate appropriate recipes online or in books. Then, make up a grocery list. Buy groceries and gather necessary materials, such as mixing bowls, spoons, and pans. Cook your characters' favorite foods by yourself or with friends.
Write a Sequel ___/___/___	What happens to the characters in your book after you finish reading the final page? Why not create a sequel? A sequel is a book that is published after the first book has enjoyed success among readers. Sequels generally pick up where the first book left off. For example, the sequel to Madeleine L'Engle's novel *A Wrinkle in Time* is *A Wind in the Door*.

Read–Together Chart

Does your father read books to you before bed? Perhaps your mother reads to the family at breakfast? Your grandparents may enjoy reading books to you after school or on the weekends. You and your family members can create a Read–Together Chart and fill it in to keep track of all the books you've read together.

Here are two Read–Together Charts. The first one is a sample. The second one has been left blank, so you can add your own categories and books.

Book We Read	Who Read It?	What It's About	Our Review
Wings of Fire Legends: Darkstalker	My mom and I take turns reading it to each other.	It's an origin story about how Darkstalker grew to become Pyrrhia's most dangerous dragon.	I love dragons, and this is so epic! It fills us in on who Darkstalker was and how the love of his life sacrificed her own happiness to protect others from him.

Learning Experiences

A continuación, se incluyen algunas actividades divertidas y de bajo costo que puedes realizar junto a tu hijo. Pronto descubrirás que las mismas pueden ser estimulantes, educativas y complementarias del resto de los ejercicios del libro.

Tarjetas didácticas __/__/__	Elabora todo tipo de tarjetas didácticas. Dependiendo de los intereses de tu hijo y su grado académico, pueden incluir letras del abecedario, palabras de uso frecuente, o problemas matemáticos. Puedes crearlas tú mismo con marcadores o en una computadora. Sugiérele que te ayude a cortar imágenes de revistas y péguenlas en tarjetas de 3" × 5". Luego, busca un sitio al aire libre y repasen las tarjetas juntos.
Proyecto de despensa __/__/__	Encuentra un sitio en tu casa donde puedas almacenar víveres. Puede ser un armario o un contenedor que permanezca siempre en el mismo sitio. Busca algunas latas de pintura limpias o baldes. Llénalos con todo tipo de materiales para hacer manualidades. Además de las clásicas pinturas, marcadores, papel, tijeras y pegamento, puedes incluir artículos inusuales, tales como azulejos, flores artificiales y papel de regalo. De este modo, cada vez tú y tu hijo quieran hacer una manualidad, pueden acceder a todo lo necesario en ese preciso momento.
¿Cuanto cuesta? __/__/__	Si salen a comer, pide ayuda a tu hijo para obtener el total de la cuenta. Anoten el costo de la comida de cada comensal. Luego, dile que lo sume y calcule cuánto se gastó en total. Puedes modificar la actividad y volverla mucho más simple, pidiéndole que sólo calcule el costo de una entrada y un trago del menú, o el costo de tres postres. Asegúrate de redondear las cifras primero.
Búsqueda del tesoro en la naturaleza __/__/__	Salgan a caminar, vayan a un parque o realicen una excursión a las montañas. Pero antes de partir, elabora una búsqueda del tesoro para tu hijo. Puede incluir todo tipo de cosas que se puedan encontrar en la naturaleza. Asegúrate que cuente con una bolsa para guardar todo lo que encuentre (y recuerda verificar con anticipación las reglas ó leyes relacionadas con la sustracción de cualquier objeto). Puedes incluir cosas tales como: una hoja con bordes puntiagudos, una roca moteada, y una ramita con dos pequeñas ramificaciones. Tómense unos minutos para observar todos los elementos que ha recolectado y táchenlos de la lista.
Realiza un viaje y lleva un diario __/__/__	Si van a realizar un viaje durante el verano, pídele a tu hijo que lleve un diario. Los niños pequeños pueden recolectar postales y pegarlas en un diario en blanco. También pueden dibujar los sitios que visitaron. Si tiene acceso a una cámara de fotos, puede armar un álbum fotográfico.

Cursive Writing Chart

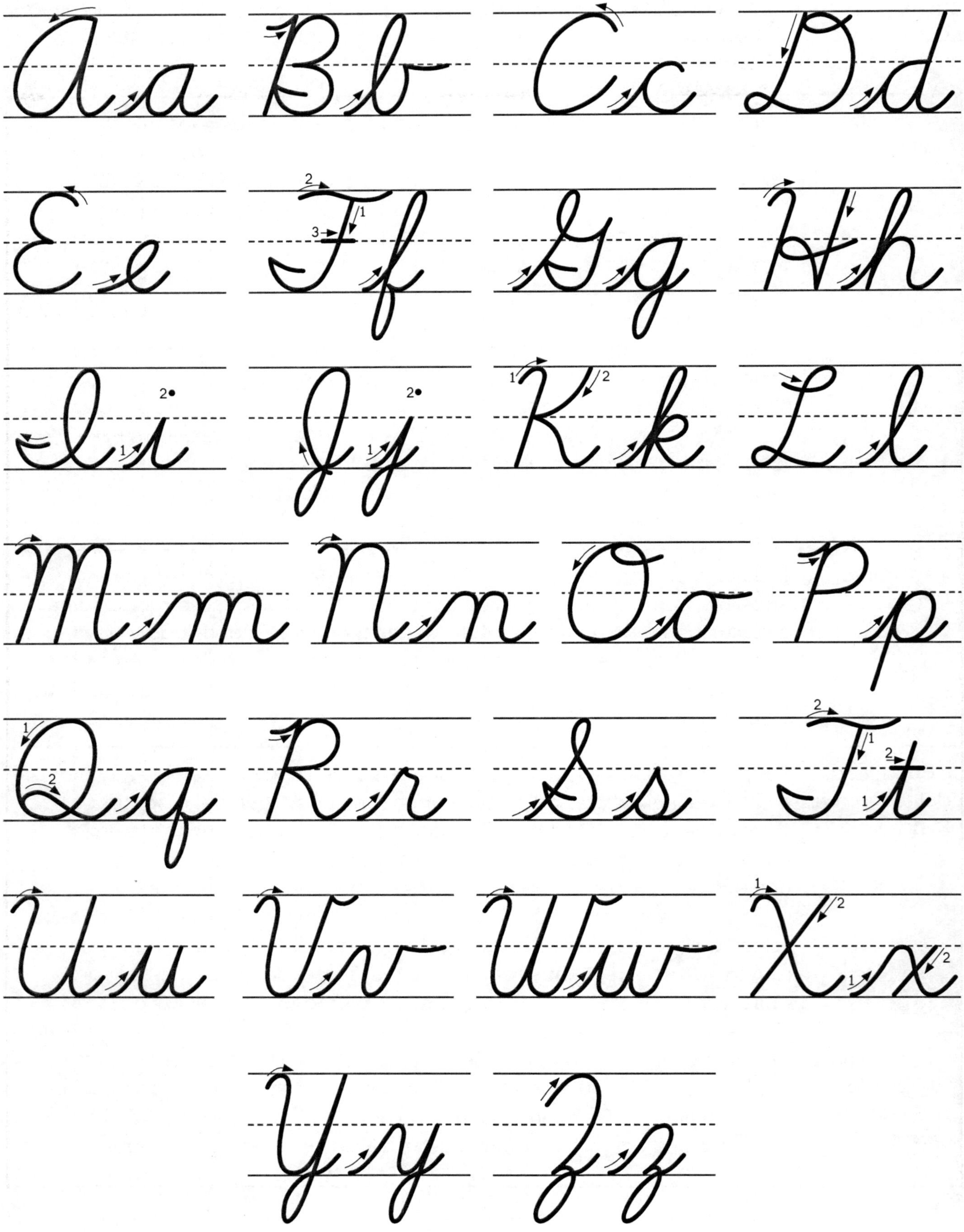

Multiplication Chart

×	0	1	2	3	4	5	6	7	8	9	10	11	12
0	0	0	0	0	0	0	0	0	0	0	0	0	0
1	0	1	2	3	4	5	6	7	8	9	10	11	12
2	0	2	4	6	8	10	12	14	16	18	20	22	24
3	0	3	6	9	12	15	18	21	24	27	30	33	36
4	0	4	8	12	16	20	24	28	32	36	40	44	48
5	0	5	10	15	20	25	30	35	40	45	50	55	60
6	0	6	12	18	24	30	36	42	48	54	60	66	72
7	0	7	14	21	28	35	42	49	56	63	70	77	84
8	0	8	16	24	32	40	48	56	64	72	80	88	96
9	0	9	18	27	36	45	54	63	72	81	90	99	108
10	0	10	20	30	40	50	60	70	80	90	100	110	120
11	0	11	22	33	44	55	66	77	88	99	110	121	132
12	0	12	24	36	48	60	72	84	96	108	120	132	144

Times Tables

1 times table	2 times table	3 times table
1 × 0 = 0	2 × 0 = 0	3 × 0 = 0
1 × 1 = 1	2 × 1 = 2	3 × 1 = 3
1 × 2 = 2	2 × 2 = 4	3 × 2 = 6
1 × 3 = 3	2 × 3 = 6	3 × 3 = 9
1 × 4 = 4	2 × 4 = 8	3 × 4 = 12
1 × 5 = 5	2 × 5 = 10	3 × 5 = 15
1 × 6 = 6	2 × 6 = 12	3 × 6 = 18
1 × 7 = 7	2 × 7 = 14	3 × 7 = 21
1 × 8 = 8	2 × 8 = 16	3 × 8 = 24
1 × 9 = 9	2 × 9 = 18	3 × 9 = 27
1 × 10 = 10	2 × 10 = 20	3 × 10 = 30
1 × 11 = 11	2 × 11 = 22	3 × 11 = 33
1 × 12 = 12	2 × 12 = 24	3 × 12 = 36

4 times table	5 times table	6 times table
4 × 0 = 0	5 × 0 = 0	6 × 0 = 0
4 × 1 = 4	5 × 1 = 5	6 × 1 = 6
4 × 2 = 8	5 × 2 = 10	6 × 2 = 12
4 × 3 = 12	5 × 3 = 15	6 × 3 = 18
4 × 4 = 16	5 × 4 = 20	6 × 4 = 24
4 × 5 = 20	5 × 5 = 25	6 × 5 = 30
4 × 6 = 24	5 × 6 = 30	6 × 6 = 36
4 × 7 = 28	5 × 7 = 35	6 × 7 = 42
4 × 8 = 32	5 × 8 = 40	6 × 8 = 48
4 × 9 = 36	5 × 9 = 45	6 × 9 = 54
4 × 10 = 40	5 × 10 = 50	6 × 10 = 60
4 × 11 = 44	5 × 11 = 55	6 × 11 = 66
4 × 12 = 48	5 × 12 = 60	6 × 12 = 72

Times Tables *(cont.)*

7 times table

7 × 0 = 0
7 × 1 = 7
7 × 2 = 14
7 × 3 = 21
7 × 4 = 28
7 × 5 = 35
7 × 6 = 42
7 × 7 = 49
7 × 8 = 56
7 × 9 = 63
7 × 10 = 70
7 × 11 = 77
7 × 12 = 84

8 times table

8 × 0 = 0
8 × 1 = 8
8 × 2 = 16
8 × 3 = 24
8 × 4 = 32
8 × 5 = 40
8 × 6 = 48
8 × 7 = 56
8 × 8 = 64
8 × 9 = 72
8 × 10 = 80
8 × 11 = 88
8 × 12 = 96

9 times table

9 × 0 = 0
9 × 1 = 9
9 × 2 = 18
9 × 3 = 27
9 × 4 = 36
9 × 5 = 45
9 × 6 = 54
9 × 7 = 63
9 × 8 = 72
9 × 9 = 81
9 × 10 = 90
9 × 11 = 99
9 × 12 = 108

10 times table

10 × 0 = 0
10 × 1 = 10
10 × 2 = 20
10 × 3 = 30
10 × 4 = 40
10 × 5 = 50
10 × 6 = 60
10 × 7 = 70
10 × 8 = 80
10 × 9 = 90
10 × 10 = 100
10 × 11 = 110
10 × 12 = 120

11 times table

11 × 0 = 0
11 × 1 = 11
11 × 2 = 22
11 × 3 = 33
11 × 4 = 44
11 × 5 = 55
11 × 6 = 66
11 × 7 = 77
11 × 8 = 88
11 × 9 = 99
11 × 10 = 110
11 × 11 = 121
11 × 12 = 132

12 times table

12 × 0 = 0
12 × 1 = 12
12 × 2 = 24
12 × 3 = 36
12 × 4 = 48
12 × 5 = 60
12 × 6 = 72
12 × 7 = 84
12 × 8 = 96
12 × 9 = 108
12 × 10 = 120
12 × 11 = 132
12 × 12 = 144

Division Tables

Divided by 1
1 ÷ 1 = 1
2 ÷ 1 = 2
3 ÷ 1 = 3
4 ÷ 1 = 4
5 ÷ 1 = 5
6 ÷ 1 = 6
7 ÷ 1 = 7
8 ÷ 1 = 8
9 ÷ 1 = 9
10 ÷ 1 = 10
11 ÷ 1 = 11
12 ÷ 1 = 12

Divided by 2
2 ÷ 2 = 1
4 ÷ 2 = 2
6 ÷ 2 = 3
8 ÷ 2 = 4
10 ÷ 2 = 5
12 ÷ 2 = 6
14 ÷ 2 = 7
16 ÷ 2 = 8
18 ÷ 2 = 9
20 ÷ 2 = 10
22 ÷ 2 = 11
24 ÷ 2 = 12

Divided by 3
3 ÷ 3 = 1
6 ÷ 3 = 2
9 ÷ 3 = 3
12 ÷ 3 = 4
15 ÷ 3 = 5
18 ÷ 3 = 6
21 ÷ 3 = 7
24 ÷ 3 = 8
27 ÷ 3 = 9
30 ÷ 3 = 10
33 ÷ 3 = 11
36 ÷ 3 = 12

Divided by 4
4 ÷ 4 = 1
8 ÷ 4 = 2
12 ÷ 4 = 3
16 ÷ 4 = 4
20 ÷ 4 = 5
24 ÷ 4 = 6
28 ÷ 4 = 7
32 ÷ 4 = 8
36 ÷ 4 = 9
40 ÷ 4 = 10
44 ÷ 4 = 11
48 ÷ 4 = 12

Divided by 5
5 ÷ 5 = 1
10 ÷ 5 = 2
15 ÷ 5 = 3
20 ÷ 5 = 4
25 ÷ 5 = 5
30 ÷ 5 = 6
35 ÷ 5 = 7
40 ÷ 5 = 8
45 ÷ 5 = 9
50 ÷ 5 = 10
55 ÷ 5 = 11
60 ÷ 5 = 12

Divided by 6
6 ÷ 6 = 1
12 ÷ 6 = 2
18 ÷ 6 = 3
24 ÷ 6 = 4
30 ÷ 6 = 5
36 ÷ 6 = 6
42 ÷ 6 = 7
48 ÷ 6 = 8
54 ÷ 6 = 9
60 ÷ 6 = 10
66 ÷ 6 = 11
72 ÷ 6 = 12

Division Tables *(cont.)*

Divided by 7
7 ÷ 7 = 1
14 ÷ 7 = 2
21 ÷ 7 = 3
28 ÷ 7 = 4
35 ÷ 7 = 5
42 ÷ 7 = 6
49 ÷ 7 = 7
56 ÷ 7 = 8
63 ÷ 7 = 9
70 ÷ 7 = 10
77 ÷ 7 = 11
84 ÷ 7 = 12

Divided by 8
8 ÷ 8 = 1
16 ÷ 8 = 2
24 ÷ 8 = 3
32 ÷ 8 = 4
40 ÷ 8 = 5
48 ÷ 8 = 6
56 ÷ 8 = 7
64 ÷ 8 = 8
72 ÷ 8 = 9
80 ÷ 8 = 10
88 ÷ 8 = 11
96 ÷ 8 = 12

Divided by 9
9 ÷ 9 = 1
18 ÷ 9 = 2
27 ÷ 9 = 3
36 ÷ 9 = 4
45 ÷ 9 = 5
54 ÷ 9 = 6
63 ÷ 9 = 7
72 ÷ 9 = 8
81 ÷ 9 = 9
90 ÷ 9 = 10
99 ÷ 9 = 11
108 ÷ 9 = 12

Divided by 10
10 ÷ 10 = 1
20 ÷ 10 = 2
30 ÷ 10 = 3
40 ÷ 10 = 4
50 ÷ 10 = 5
60 ÷ 10 = 6
70 ÷ 10 = 7
80 ÷ 10 = 8
90 ÷ 10 = 9
100 ÷ 10 = 10
110 ÷ 10 = 11
120 ÷ 10 = 12

Divided by 11
11 ÷ 11 = 1
22 ÷ 11 = 2
33 ÷ 11 = 3
44 ÷ 11 = 4
55 ÷ 11 = 5
66 ÷ 11 = 6
77 ÷ 11 = 7
88 ÷ 11 = 8
99 ÷ 11 = 9
110 ÷ 11 = 10
121 ÷ 11 = 11
132 ÷ 11 = 12

Divided by 12
12 ÷ 12 = 1
24 ÷ 12 = 2
36 ÷ 12 = 3
48 ÷ 12 = 4
60 ÷ 12 = 5
72 ÷ 12 = 6
84 ÷ 12 = 7
96 ÷ 12 = 8
108 ÷ 12 = 9
120 ÷ 12 = 10
132 ÷ 12 = 11
144 ÷ 12 = 12

Proofreading Marks

Editor's Mark	Meaning	Example
≡	capitalize	they fished in lake tahoe.
/	make it lowercase	Five Students missed the Bus.
sp.	spelling mistake	The day was clowdy and cold.
⊙	add a period	Tomorrow is a holiday
ℓ	delete (remove)	One person knew the the answer.
∧	add a word	Six were in the litter. (pups)
∧,	add a comma	He planted peas corn, and squash.
∽	reverse words or letters	An otter swam in the bed kelp.
∨'	add an apostrophe	The childs bike was blue.
∨" ∨"	add quotation marks	Why can't I go? she cried.
#	make a space	He ate two redapples.
⁀ ‿	close the space	Her favorite game is soft ball.
¶	begin a new paragraph	to know. Next on the list

Answer Key

Page 12

1. $193.05
2. $12.09
3. $83.70
4. $11.99
5. $11.16
6. $250.00

Page 13

1. provides moisture, cleans the eye
2. a. 75, b. 70, c. 60
3. computer use means less blinking, which means less moisture and cleaning

Page 14

1. Art Supplies: $2.00
   Snacks: $3.00
   Clothes: $4.00
   Savings: $1.00
2. $4.00
3. $2.00 x 52 = $104.00
4. 7 weeks

Page 15

Main Idea: The most well-known periodic comet is Halley's Comet.

Supporting Detail: It makes regular passes by Earth.

Supporting Detail: It can be seen every 75 years or so.

Page 16

1928 – pre-sliced bread
1929 – sunglasses
1941 – O-shaped cereal
1967 – handheld calculator
1989 – World Wide Web
1992 – smartphone

Page 17

1. muscles
2. kayak
3. exhausted
4. navigate
5. collapse
6. d
7. a
8. b
9. c
10. e

Page 18

1. Cost = $3.74; Change = $1.26
2. Cost = $4.98; Change = $0.02
3. Cost = $4.97; Change = $5.03
4. Cost = $8.48; Change = $1.52
5. Cost = $11.97; Change = $8.03

Page 20

2. dew
3. wind
4. icy
5. season
6. sun
7. storm
8. heat
9. rain
10. thunder
11. cloud
12. tornado

Page 22

1. 48
2. 41
3. a. 59, b. 2017, c. NL
4. a. 36, b. 2013, c. NL
5. 2017 and 2019

Page 23

A Crow named pete r Lee lived in st Louis, missouri. One tuesday in july, Pete wanted a drink of water. the only water was at the bottom of a pitcher, and Pete couldn't reach it How could Pete drink? Pete picked up a little Pebble with his Beak and dropped it in the pitcher. Pete did this over and over until the water level was high enough for him to drink

Page 24

1. 56 feet
2. 45 feet
3. 60 meters
4. 50 meters
5. 46 meters
6. 40 meters

Page 25

4, 2, 1, 6, 3, 5

Answer Key (cont.)

Page 26

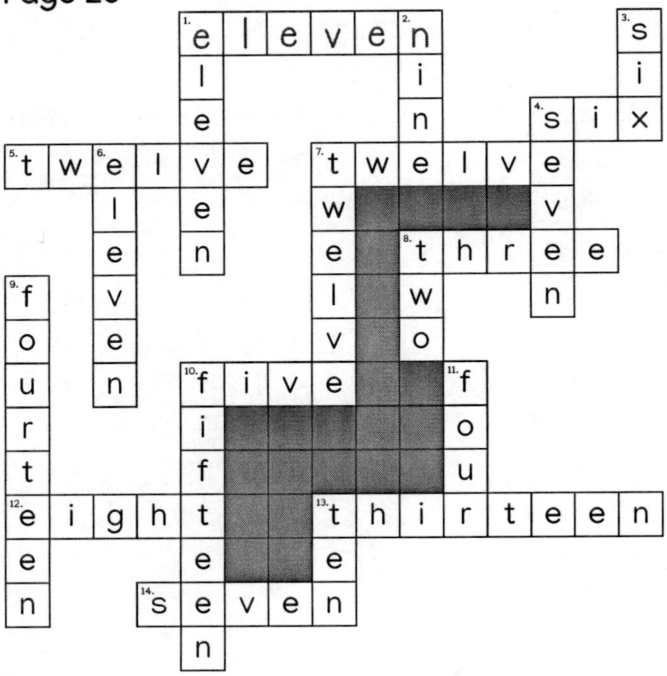

Page 28

1. $\frac{3}{4}$ lb. ground beef
   $1\frac{1}{4}$ lbs. beans
   1 lb. tomatoes
   $\frac{1}{2}$ lb. macaroni
   1 oz. chili pepper
   $1\frac{1}{2}$ oz. hot sauce
   5 oz. tomato sauce
   4 oz. water

2. 1 lb. ground beef
   $1\frac{2}{3}$ lbs. beans
   $1\frac{1}{3}$ lbs. tomatoes
   $\frac{2}{3}$ lb. macaroni
   $1\frac{1}{3}$ oz. chili pepper
   2 oz. hot sauce
   $6\frac{2}{3}$ oz. tomato sauce
   $5\frac{1}{3}$ oz. water

3. $1\frac{1}{2}$ lbs. ground beef
   $2\frac{1}{2}$ lbs. beans
   2 lbs. tomatoes
   1 lb. macaroni
   2 oz. chili pepper
   3 oz. hot sauce
   10 oz. tomato sauce
   8 oz. water

Page 29

1. d **2.** d **3.** b

Page 30

1. Sean eats hot dogs and drinks milk.
2. Jay eats hamburgers and drinks shakes.
3. Tina eats tacos and drinks water.
4. Marie eats pizza and drinks soda.

Page 31

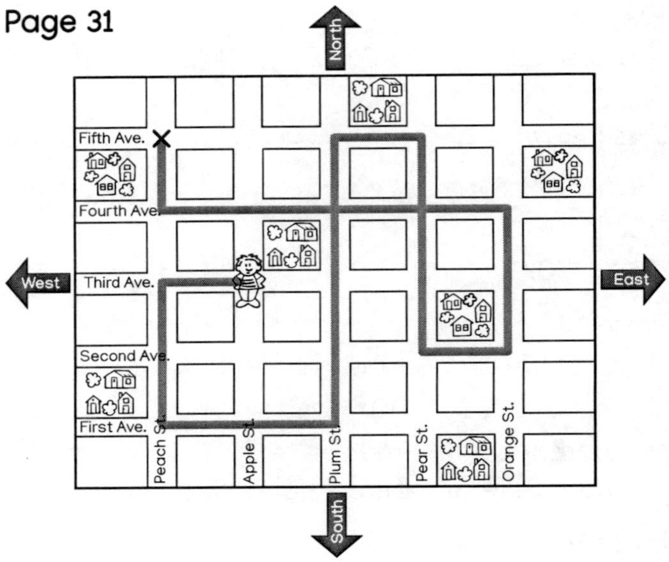

Page 32

1. C, \$475 **3.** $\frac{8}{15}$ **5.** 36, 6
2. $\frac{4}{30}$ or $\frac{2}{15}$ **4.** $\frac{3}{8}$ **6.** $\frac{48}{54}$ or $\frac{8}{9}$

Page 33

1. d **2.** d **3.** b **4.** a

Page 34

1. d **2.** b **3.** b **4.** 67 and 77

Page 36

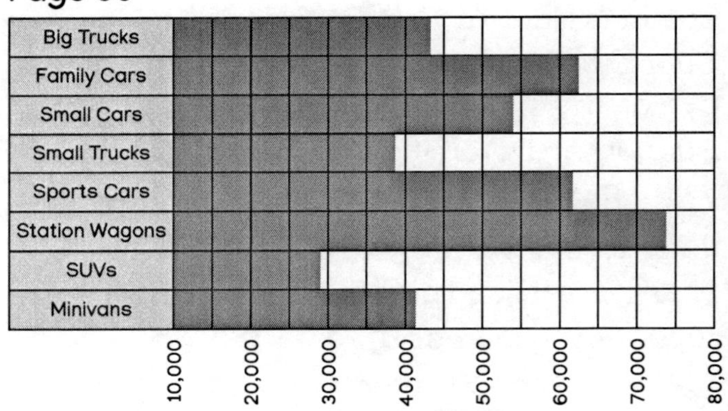

1. 81,341 **5.** 9,154
2. 116,415 **6.** 7,502
3. 91,060 **7.** 18,790
4. 71,005 **8.** 32,013

Page 37

1. c **3.** b **5.** b **7.** c
2. a **4.** a **6.** c **8.** a

Page 38

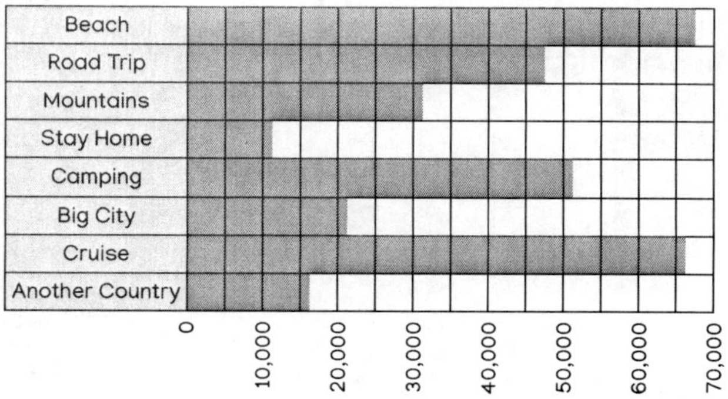

1. 78,696
2. 83,912
3. 68,601
4. 81,681
5. 22,260
6. 15,000
7. 3,125
8. 30,311

Page 40

Make a difference today!
Listen and learn.

Page 41

1. banana split
2. Robin Hood
3. Ring Around the Rosie
4. I understand.
5. Once upon a time

Page 42

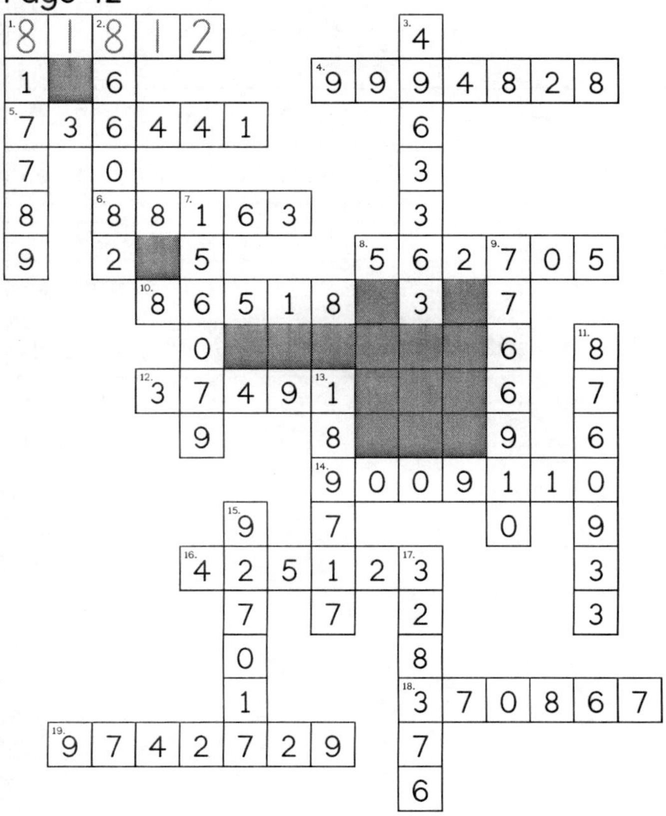

Page 43

1. b
2. a
3. e
4. d
5. c

Page 44

1. $44.24
2. $14.64
3. $37.17
4. $54.39
5. $36.74
6. $18.00
7. $14.64
8. $19.92
9. $55.56
10. $33.28
11. $54.39
12. $33.75
13. $59.49
14. $93.99
15. $73.92
16. $14.64
17. $18.00
18. $14.64
19. $80.96
20. $18.00
21. $14.64

Answer: because it had more sense

Page 45

1. b
2. d
3. b
4. a

Page 46

1. David Peterson
2. $5.80, Kat Ross
3. Barbara Marshall
4. no
5. no
6. 553
7. $43.00

Page 48

1. Checkers
2. Old Maid
3. 5
4. 6
5. 20
6. 4
7. 19
8. 44

Page 49

B. 1, 3, 5, 2, 4
C. 4, 2, 1, 5, 3
D. 3, 2, 4, 1, 5
E. 5, 4, 2, 1, 3
F. 3, 5, 1, 2, 4
G. 2, 1, 4, 3, 5
H. 3, 5, 1, 2, 4

Page 50

2. 26 letters in the alphabet
3. 52 weeks in a year
4. Thomas Edison invented the light bulb.
5. 4 quarters in a dollar (or 4 queens in a deck)
6. 7 continents on planet Earth
7. At 32 degrees, water freezes.
8. George Washington was the first president.

Answer Key *(cont.)*

Page 51

2. camel
3. dog
4. goat
5. fish
6. owl
7. seal
8. cat
9. bear
10. deer
11. lion
12. hen
13. oyster
14. horse
15. hippo

Page 52

1. 50
2. 10
3. 25
4. 45
5. soccer, basketball
6. swimming, bicycling
7. 45
8. 20

Page 53

1. b
2. c
3. a
4. c

Page 54

1. mall
2. school
3. bank
4. III
5. I
6. (3, –8)
7. library
8. park

Page 55

1. so
2. but
3. but
4. and
5. so

6–8. Answers will vary.

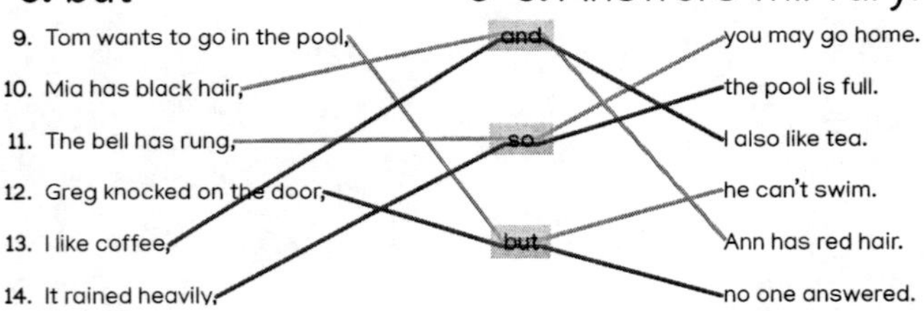

Page 56

1. 135 sq. feet
2. 98 sq. feet
3. 24 sq. feet
4. 104 sq. feet
5. 192 sq. feet
6. 72 sq. feet

Page 57

1. four
2. bear
3. passed
4. it's
5. Who's
6. led
7. peace
8. their, two
9. fair, fare
10. right, write, rite

Page 58

1. d
2.

Day	Mon.	Tues.	Wed.	Thurs.	Total Minutes
Minutes	45	50	75	50	220

3. c
4. b

Page 59

5. fact
6. fact
7. opinion
8. opinion

Page 61

ZOO

Page 62

Monthly Billing Item	Monthly Amount	Yearly Amount
Home	$1,522.45	**$18,269.40**
Cable TV	$75.40	**$904.80**
Electricity	$120.34	**$1,444.08**
Gas	$60.52	**$726.24**
Telephone	$68.95	**$827.40**
Cars	$650.39	**$7,804.68**
Food	$200.85	**$2,410.20**
Clothing	$102.09	**$1,225.08**
	Total Yearly Expenditures	**$33,611.88**

1. $546.00
2. $37.70
3. $452.40
4. $2,170.32
5. $1,185.12

Answer Key *(cont.)*

Page 63

asia	england	murray river	south	uranus
insects	kansas city	october	stranger	vietnam
canada	london	pacific ocean	summer	wattle street
christmas	michelle	plate	swan lake	wednesday
easter	mount everest	shamrock hotel	tables	white house

8. Last Saturday Julie went to Chicago.
9. At Christmas, we are going to Italy, which is a country in Europe.
10. The wedding will take place at St. Patrick's Church in Greensboro.

Page 64

1. $8,400; no
2. $4,080; yes
3. $7,506.60; yes
4. Apartments B and C; $3,426.60

Page 65

2. minibus
3. mini terrier
4. minivan
5. microwave
6. microscope
8. miniskirt
9. microfilm
10. microphone
11. minute
12. microscope
13. microbe
14. mini terrier

Page 66

1. 90°
2. 120°
3. 90°
4. 110°
5. 110°
6. 120°
7. 125°
8. 80°
9. 95°
10. 130°
11. 100°
12. 60°

Page 68

1. 44 ft.
2. 51 m
3. 51 yds.
4. 58 cm
5. 24 cm
6. 210 m
7. 220 in.
8. 153 ft.

Page 69

1. Corn, rice, and wheat
2. Daffodils, roses, and tulips
3. Penguins, skunks, and zebras
4. Hammers, pliers, and scissors
5. Ash, oak, and sycamore
7. a Swedish astronomer
8. a featureless spot in a freezing wilderness
9. according to a 17th-century encyclopedia
10. one of this class's finest writers

Page 70

Ellis—5th place
Liza—6th place
Ben—4th place
Dan—3rd place
Paul—2nd place
Emma—1st place

Page 71

A	B	O	V	E	P	I	N	T	O
R	E	V	D	N	I	H	E	B	U
O	L	E	R	N	G	E	A	P	T
U	O	R	S	U	O	S	R	I	S
N	W	I	O	F	F	T	I	O	I
D	D	R	A	C	R	O	S	S	D
E	H	N	S	B	E	S	I	D	E
T	U	N	D	E	R	E	T	F	A

What's Left? PREPOSITIONS

Page 72

1. 1,403
2. 237,970
3. 2,202
4. 80,918
5. $47.00
6. 1,000,000+ 200,000 + 50,000 + 6,000 + 700 + 50 + 3
7. 30,000 + 8,000 + 200 + 80 + 1
8. 20,000 + 2,000 + 600
9. 800,000 + 40,000 + 3
10. 5 weeks

Page 73

2. nonfiction
3. fiction
4. fiction
5. nonfiction
6. fiction
7. Instructional
8. Informative

Page 74

1. 120°
2. 40°
3. 168°
4. 95°
5. 45¢
6. 23
7. 19
8. 11
9. 37
10. 520 miles

Answer Key *(cont.)*

Page 75

Possible examples:

1. "world at her feet"; everything was available to her
2. "time to stand on her own two feet"; take care of herself without help from others
3. "threw caution to the wind"; took a chance without worrying what would happen as a result
4. "thinking on her feet"; figuring things out quickly as they happen
5. "land on her feet"; be okay and do well

Page 76

1. 100	**6.** 6
2. 7	**7.** 44
3. 12	**8.** 2
4. 81	**9.** 92
5. Mrs. Baker's	**10.** 1607

Page 77

1. strait	**7.** e
2. hydroplane	**8.** c
3. isthmus	**9.** b
4. delta	**10.** d
5. hydroelectric	**11.** f
6. tributary	**12.** a

Page 78

2. <	**5.** <	**8.** >	**11.** >
3. >	**6.** <	**9.** <	**12.** >
4. <	**7.** >	**10.** <	

Page 79

Person: cousin, girl, student
Place: Houston, Spain, country
Thing: book, cat, desk
Idea: happiness, love, wisdom

Page 80

2. rivers, lakes, seas
3. tuck, pike, straight
4. bathing suit, goggles
5. speed and stamina
6. Never swim alone.

Page 81

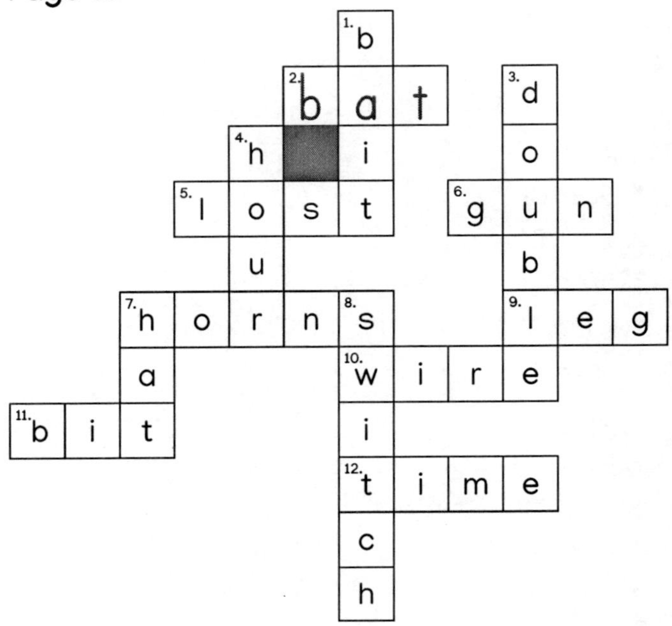

Page 82

1. 90	**6.** 45
2. 25	**7.** 300
3. 70	**8.** $220,000
4. 25	**9.** $110,000
5. 45	**10.** $50,000

Page 84

Party Fruit Salad
Serves 24 people
18 cups watermelon
6 cups raisins
9 apples
$1\frac{1}{2}$ cups cherries
3 mangoes
Rule: Multiply by 3.

Turkey Loaf
Serves 64 people
16 lbs. ground turkey
40 tbsp. breadcrumbs
$2\frac{2}{3}$ cups onions
8 eggs
8 dashes salt
8 dashes pepper
Rule: Multiply by 8.

Chili
Serves 4 people
4 oz. cooked black beans
8 oz. cooked kidney beans
$\frac{1}{6}$ tsp. fresh garlic
$\frac{1}{10}$ lb. snap beans
$\frac{1}{2}$ package chili powder
$\frac{1}{2}$ cup salsa
Rule: Divide by 2 or multiply by $\frac{1}{2}$.

Page 86

1. 64 cm^3
2. 1,000 $ft.^3$
3. 1,728 m^3
4. 343 mm^3
5. 729 $ft.^3$
6. 512 cm^3
7. 8,000 mm^3
8. 15,625 $ft.^3$
9. 125,000 cm^3
10. 10,648 cm^3

Page 88

1.
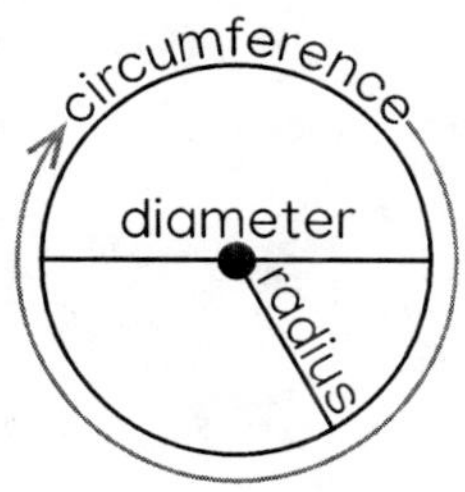

2.
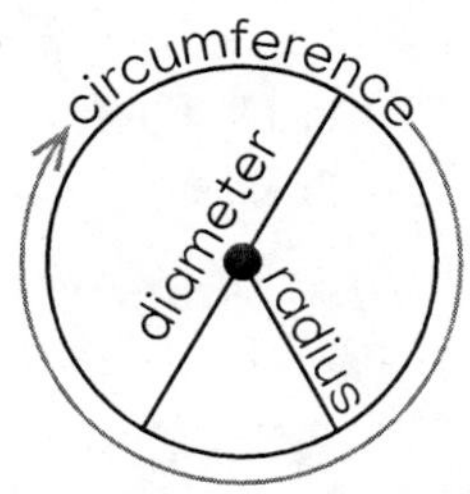

3.
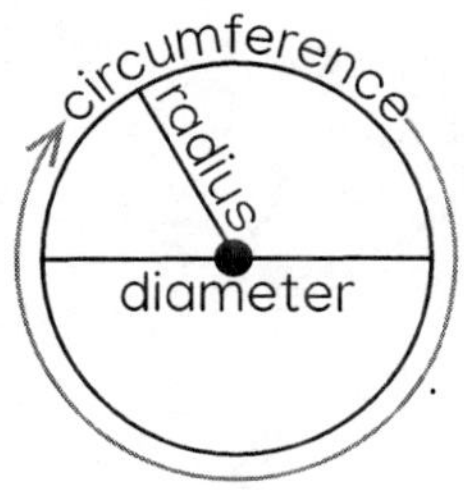

4.
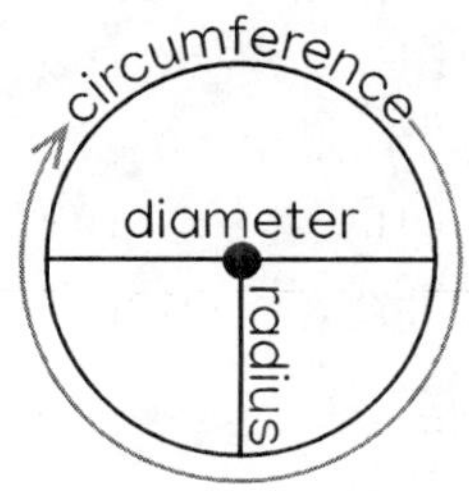

5. r = 7 ft.
   d = 14 ft.
   C = 44 ft.
6. r = 18 cm
   d = 36 cm
   C = 113 cm
7. r = 11 cm
   d = 22 cm
   C = 69 cm
8. r = 21 in.
   d = 42 in.
   C = 132 in.

Page 89

1. Paragraph #2: to tell what the story is about; Paragraph #3: to give ideas about why we may yawn; Paragraph #4: to tell another mystery about yawning

Page 90

This soccer player was born in **Brazil.** At age fifteen, he played for the **Santos,** a professional soccer club. He was a talented **forward** and led his team to three **world** championships. He **retired** in 1973, but in 1975, he returned to play for the New York **Cosmos.** The full name of this amazing athlete is **Edson Arantes do Nascimento,** but he is best known by his nickname, **Pele.**

Reward Chart